THE BEST OF
YELLOWSTONE
NATIONAL PARK

by ALAN LEFTRIDGE

FARCOUNTRY
PRESS

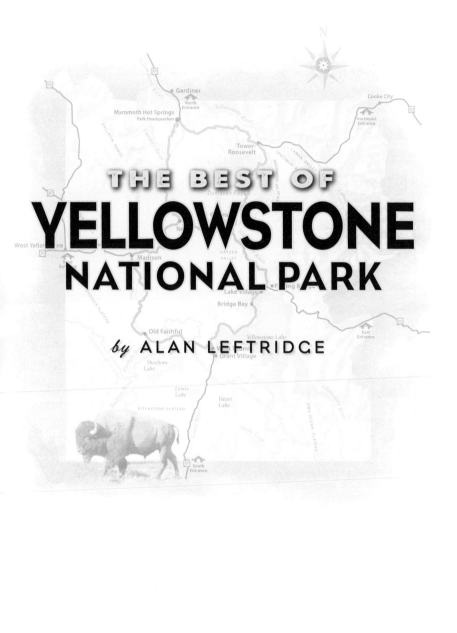

THE BEST OF
YELLOWSTONE
NATIONAL PARK

by ALAN LEFTRIDGE

ISBN 10: 1-56037-599-X
ISBN 13: 978-1-56037-599-9

Cover photograph © Ann and Rob Simpson
Inset bison photograph © Linda Duvanich

All photographs by Alan Leftridge except where credited otherwise.

For more information about our books, write Farcountry Press, P.O. Box 5630,
Helena, MT 59604; call (800) 821-3874; or visit www.farcountrypress.com.

Library of Congress Cataloging-in-Publication Data

Leftridge, Alan.
   The best of Yellowstone National Park / by Alan Leftridge.
      pages cm. – (The best of)
   ISBN-13: 978-1-56037-599-9
   ISBN-10: 1-56037-599-X
   1. Yellowstone National Park–Guidebooks. I. Title.
   F722.L37 2014
   978.7'52–dc23
                                        2014004736

 Created, produced, designed, and printed in the United States.

18   17   16   15   14   1   2   3   4   5

PREFACE

"We're here! What is there to do?"

I heard this exclamation and question many times while working as an interpretive park ranger at the Albright Visitor Center in Mammoth. Visitors were excited that they had arrived and wanted to start making memories, in what early day promoters called "Wonderland."

"What is there to do?" is a question that you might ask a park employee or a friend. But you may have neither person to ask as you schedule your vacation. With limited time, it is best to plan your visit so that you are able to take in the locations that others have found most symbolic of the park.

The purpose of this book is to reveal Yellowstone National Park's iconic features, and to relate to you the best of the park as identified by some of the people who work and live here. I intend to do this by telling you what I think you should know about the park, as if you were a family member or friend visiting the park for the first time.

So, this book is for you. To encourage you to experience the wonder, wildness, and ongoing changes that can be found in Yellowstone National Park, through sightseeing, hiking, wildlife viewing, wildflower admiration, painting, photographing, and learning its natural and cultural history. These stories and experiences will lead you to the essence of "Wonderland."

Alan Leftridge
Swan Valley, Montana

HOW TO USE THE MAPS IN THIS BOOK

BEST PLACES TO SEE WILDLIFE FROM THE ROAD

The maps in this book show numbered locations for features and activities described in each chapter. Some indicate general areas, while others show more specific locations for individual subjects explained in the text. Use these maps with the more detailed visitor map you receive at any entrance station. For hiking and backpacking, even more detailed topographic maps are recommended, available at vendors throughout the park.

AMERICA'S LEGACY

W. H. Jackson, U.S. Geological Survey

Think about the parts of our culture that we prize: our judicial system, representative democracy, freedom of will, and economic mobility. All of these were assimilated from other cultures. One treasure that America has gifted others is the national park concept. Yellowstone is the world's first national park. When Congress passed *An Act to Set Apart a Certain Tract of Land Lying Near the Headwaters of the Yellowstone River as a Public Park*, in 1872, it was expressing the highest plane of democracy: setting aside public land for generations yet unborn. Many nations now have national parks. The idea was inspired here, in Yellowstone.

WHERE'S YELLOWSTONE?

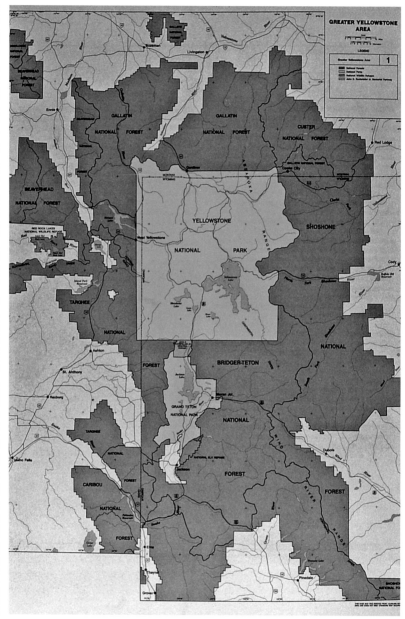

National Park Service

Look at the official park map the ranger gives you at the entrance station. Notice that the park boundaries are straight lines in some places or follow mountain ridges in others. The park borders come from administrative agreements.

Consider the habitat ranges of Yellowstone's fauna and flora. For example, the park's official flower, the fringed gentian, is found growing throughout the Northwest, not just in the park. In winter, elk and bison are drawn to lower elevations beyond park boundaries. Grizzly bears and black bears are found throughout the region, freely wandering between the park and the surrounding national forests. Neither plants nor animals respond to subjective boundaries.

So, where's Yellowstone? It is at the heart of an 18-million-acre landscape known as the Greater Yellowstone Ecosystem. Politically unbounded, the GYE covers almost a third of Wyoming, much of south-central Montana, and a slice of eastern Idaho to the Snake River plain. This is a multifaceted, intertwining organization of plants, animals, and humans, with a volcano at its heart.

Jim Peaco, National Park Service

YELLOWSTONE: JUST THE FACTS

Jim Peaco, National Park Service

- Yellowstone is the world's first national park, established in 1872.

- Yellowstone National Park is 2,221,766 acres, equal to 3,472 square miles, the combined size of Rhode Island and Delaware.

- Ninety-six percent of the park is in Wyoming, three percent in Montana, and one percent in Idaho.
- Three of the park's entrances are in Montana, two in Wyoming, and one in Idaho.
- Annual visitation exceeds 3 million people, with July the busiest month and March the quietest.
- The park's highest point is Eagle Peak in the southeast corner at 11,358 feet. The lowest point is where Reese Creek leaves the park, northwest of the North Entrance, at 5,282 feet. Yellowstone's average elevation is 8,000 feet.
- About 5 percent of the park is covered by water, 15 percent is grassland, and 80 percent is forested land.
- The 1988 fires affected about 36 percent of the park—mostly the forested areas.
- Precipitation ranges from 10 inches at the north boundary to 80 inches in the southwest corner.
- The average daytime January temperature at Mammoth is 9°F; in July the average daytime temperature is 80°F.
- Record high and low temperatures: 99°F in 2002 at Mammoth Hot Springs, -66°F in 1933 at the West Entrance.
- Yellowstone National Park contains an active volcano that is responsible for 1,000 to 3,000 earthquakes annually.
- The volcano created one of the world's largest calderas, measuring 30 by 45 miles.
- The park has more than 10,000 geothermal features, including 300 geysers.
- Within the geothermal features live at least 406 species of thermophiles.
- Yellowstone National Park has 290 waterfalls that flow year-round. The tallest is the Lower Falls of the Yellowstone River at 308 feet.
- Yellowstone Lake boasts 131.7 square miles of surface area, with 141 miles of shoreline and a maximum depth of 410 feet.

🐟 Although Teddy Roosevelt was a supporter of the national park idea, he was not responsible for the establishment of Yellowstone. His influences came a quarter of a century after the park was established. President Ulysses S. Grant signed the law that became known as the Yellowstone Park Act in 1872.

🐟 For a brief time, the Yellowstone area was known as Colter's Hell. But the geothermal area mountain man John Colter described is actually just west of Cody, Wyoming, along the North Fork Highway (U.S. 14/16/20). As you drive through Shoshone Canyon downstream from Buffalo Bill Dam, look for 30-foot extinct geyser cones on the rim above the road and hot springs bubbling on the river's edge below.

🐟 There was a group of Native Americans who lived year-round in Yellowstone, a small band of Sheepeater Shoshoni. According to Shoshone tribal people, other bands lived in Yellowstone on a seasonal basis.

- In the park's early years, Superintendent Norris worried that tourists' anxieties about Indians would discourage them from visiting Yellowstone. He circulated a myth that native people feared the geothermal features and thus avoided the park. In reality, Native Americans were not afraid of the geothermal features but instead revered, respected, or were indifferent to them. It was Anglo-Americans who gave geothermal features ominous names like Colter's Hell, Devil's Den, and Black Dragon's Cauldron. Look for features with similar names as you tour the park.

- Although wildlife were plentiful, indigenous people did not need to rely only on Yellowstone's resources for sustenance. Most of their needs were found within their homelands, which included the park and areas beyond. For example, tribal people from present-day Idaho ventured through Yellowstone to the buffalo grounds in eastern Montana and Wyoming along the Bannock Trail and other routes.

- It is probable that Yellowstone—the river and the park—were named for rock formations at the confluence of the Yellowstone and Missouri Rivers near Montana's eastern border with North Dakota. Roche Jaune, the French word for Yellowstone that fur trappers used, was a literal translation of the Minnetaree Indian term, *Mi tsi a-da-zi.*

- Yellowstone is a federal reservation with its own magistrate, courthouse, and jail, all in Mammoth.

- Yellowstone contains approximately half of the world's geothermal features. There are over 10,000 geothermal features, including about 300 geysers, in the park.

- Roads and facilities take up about three percent of the park's 2.25 million acres. The rest is wilderness.

- With the exception of the black-footed ferret, all of the major animal species that were present in Yellowstone at the time of the signing of the Declaration of Independence are represented in the park today.

Jim Peaco, National Park Service

YELLOWSTONE'S CLIMATE AND WEATHER

Jim Peaco, National Park Service

Local residents quip that Yellowstone has only two seasons: winter and July. Indeed, snow and cold weather can occur any month of the year. So, what is the climate like and what sort of weather should you expect during your visit?

Climate is day-to-day weather averaged over a long period. Yellowstone's present climate is characterized by mild summer days with cool nights and cold winters with daily maximum temperatures at or below freezing. Autumn is a short, cool, and dry season, and springtime is a long transitional season where snow lingers into June in the high country.

Climate information for Yellowstone is based on systematic weather observations that began at Mammoth Hot Springs in 1890 by the U.S. Army, and continues today. Results have stayed fairly consistent. You can expect July daytime temperatures ranging between 70°F and 80°F, and nighttime temperatures falling below 40°F. The record high temperature was recorded at 99°F in 2002 at Mammoth.

Prepare for extreme low temperatures if you visit during winter. The West Entrance, at Riverside Station, recorded -66°F in 1933. It is common to have several days in succession where -20°F is the daytime high! The average low temperature in January is 1°F, with the average high at 24°F.

Snow accumulation may begin in October, and snow stays on the ground until early April. The average duration of snow cover is about 240 days for the average park elevation of 8,000 feet; this duration varies with elevation.

For up-to-date weather information, go to www.nps.gov/yell.

A SHORT CULTURAL HISTORY OF YELLOWSTONE

National Park Service

People have been here a long time. We know that because among the park's cultural resources are 1,600 archeological sites. Native Americans were hunting, traveling through, and visiting the Yellowstone region at least 10,000 years ago.

Adventure and fur trapping brought French-Canadians and Euro-Americans to the region by the 1800s. John Colter, Jim Bridger, Osborne Russell, and others shared stories about the wonders of the upper Yellowstone River. Their tales inspired other curious-minded people to investigate the realities of the stories.

After the Civil War, dreams of western expansion fueled interest in the region. Government explorations were mounted, including the Folsom-Cook Expedition of 1869, Washburn Expedition in 1870, and Hayden Survey of 1871. Combined, these missions collected sufficient information to inspire Congress to set apart the area as a "pleasuring-ground for the benefit and enjoyment of the people." The act became law in 1872.

You can't have a park without people, so the railroads developed visitor services and provided transportation. Touting Yellowstone as Wonderland, the Northern Pacific Railway brought tourists to Gardiner, while the Union Pacific Railway delivered visitors to West Yellowstone. In later years, automobiles replaced trains, and visitation continued to climb. Today, Yellowstone's annual visitation tops 3.4 million.

WHY WAS THE ARMY IN YELLOWSTONE?

National Park Service

The Setup
Lawmakers did not include any provisions for administrative funding when they passed the 1872 Yellowstone Park Act. Early superintendents lived in eastern cities and resided in the park only during summer. Stipends were eventually provided for the superintendent and 10 assistants. It was unclear whether the Territory of Wyoming had jurisdiction in the new federal park.

The Incident
In 1885, a Wyoming justice of the peace by the name of Hall spied an illegal, smoldering campfire in the Lower Geyser Basin. His investigation led to the guilty party. The leader of the vacationers was Congressman Lewis E. Payson, of Illinois. When Hall tried to excise a fine from Payson, he was told that Wyoming had no jurisdiction in Yellowstone. An argument ensued. Payson refused to pay the fine.

The Outcome
Infuriated by the episode, Payson returned to Washington and lobbied his colleagues on the Public Lands Committee to eliminate all funds for Yellowstone. The measure passed. The assistant superintendents abandoned Yellowstone when funding was cut. The park was left to poachers, squatters, souvenir vendors, prospectors, and despoilers of the geothermal areas.

National Park Service

The Rescue

Missouri Senator George Vest considered himself the "Self-appointed Protector of Yellowstone National Park." In 1883, he had championed a resolution that allowed the Secretary of the Interior, in time of need, to call upon the Secretary of War to administer Yellowstone. When the appropriations were cut, the Interior Secretary made the request. The U.S. Army took control of Yellowstone and deployed the cavalry to restore order there in 1886. Troops remained in the park until 1918.

A Tribute

John Muir wrote of the tenure of the cavalry in Yellowstone: "Blessings on Uncle Sam's Soldiers. They have done the job well, and every pine tree is waving its arms for joy."

BUFFALO SOLDIERS IN YELLOWSTONE

F. J. Haynes, National Park Service

Imagine riding, pushing, and carrying a one-speed, 35-pound bicycle, loaded with another 35 pounds of provisions, over 800 miles of unimproved dirt roads. That's what the "Buffalo Soldiers" of the 25th Infantry Bicycle Corps did in August 1896 as they traveled from Fort Missoula to Yellowstone. Native Americans tagged the black infantrymen with the moniker, associating the texture of their hair with a buffalo's mane.

Their Yellowstone trip was one of several rides of increasing lengths that culminated in 20 troopers traveling from Fort Missoula to St. Louis between June 14 and July 16, 1897. The purpose of the rides was to determine the effectiveness of using a bicycle in lieu of horses. The next year, the 25th Infantry Bicycle Corps was sent to Cuba to fight in the Spanish-American War, without their bicycles.

BEST HISTORIC SITES

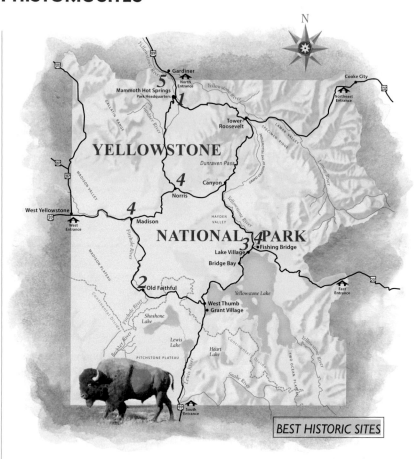

BEST HISTORIC SITES

There are 17 sites listed on the National Register of Historic Places in Yellowstone National Park. Some are buildings, like the U.S. Post Office-Yellowstone Main, while others are districts such as the North Entrance Road. Natural features like Obsidian Cliff are also recognized. The iconic sites that you don't want to miss are Fort Yellowstone, Old Faithful Inn, Lake Hotel, and Roosevelt Arch. Try to visit at least one of the three Trailside Museums.

I. Fort Yellowstone

Think about how the Mammoth area would have appeared 100 years ago. The large cottonwood trees you see now had not begun growing.

The field in front of Officer's Row was a cavalry parade ground void of roads, trees, and sinkholes. The initial fort of 1886 was on the hill just east of Mammoth Hot Springs. Fear of fire led to a fort constructed of stone. Changes have been minor since 1900; a cavalryman of that era would recognize it

National Park Service

today as his post. Visit the Albright Visitor Center and begin your self-guided tour of this remnant of Yellowstone's history.

2. Old Faithful Inn

Architect Robert Reamer wanted the inn to echo Yellowstone's wildness. Studying the building may cause you to wonder, why doesn't the inn face Old Faithful? Why did Reamer make it asymmetrical? Why is the

number of dormer windows seen from the outside not the same number viewed from the inside? Enter the building and be struck by the seven-story lobby held aloft by massive tree trunks and gnarled limb-like logs. Was the architect mirroring the old-growth lodgepole pine forest from which the trees

J. P. Clum, National Park Service

were taken? What did he want you to feel, as you enter the lobby?

These questions, and a host of others, are answered during the Old Faithful Inn Tour offered throughout the summer season. Check for posted times inside the inn.

3. Lake Hotel

Park in the large adjacent lot and enter the hotel. You have entered through what was once the back door. The front of the hotel faces Yellow-

stone Lake. In times gone by, visitors arrived by stagecoach along the road in front, or by steamer from West Thumb. Look for the old boathouse along the shore, west of the hotel.

The interior looks modern for the oldest hotel in the National Park System. The clean lines of Colonial architecture provide a classic design, a reflection of how prosperity was defined by architect Robert Reamer in 1903-1904. The hotel entertained travelers accustomed to elegance. Many aspects of the hotel are upgraded, but some things have not changed: evenings in the lobby to enjoy refreshments, and music from a string quartet or classical pianist.

4. Trailside Museums

"Roofless museums of nature" where signage and labels were thought to be intrusions. That is how Hermon Bumpus, first president of the American Association of Museums, saw parks. He endorsed

trailside museums, where exhibits focused on the immediate area, leaving the environment uncluttered. Yellowstone embarked on the construction of trailside museums from 1929 to 1932.

Architect Herbert Maier felt that buildings were a visual insult in Yellowstone and advanced a National Park Service Rustic motif. Later dubbed parkitecture, it blends the natural elements of the immediate environment into the structures. Four trailside museums were built in Yellowstone: Old Faithful in 1929, Norris in 1930, Madison in 1930, and Fishing Bridge in 1932. Old Faithful was removed in 1972, but the others remain. Visit them for the natural history stories interpreted within and become acquainted with this unique architecture.

Madison Trailside Museum
The building is located on a riverbank above the confluence of the Firehole and Gibbon Rivers as they form the Madison. The museum hosts interpretive displays about the park's history, a Yellowstone Association bookstore, and Junior Ranger activities.

Fishing Bridge Trailside Museum
This museum reveals how natural history was interpreted long ago. The bird specimens were installed in 1931. The river otters help you imagine how they exist in the wild. There is also a large, three-dimensional map that interprets the bottom of Yellowstone Lake. Exit through the back of the museum to a long, sandy beach on the lake. Gaze at the shifting medley of colors as the sunlight plays on this magnificent lake.

Norris Trailside Museum
Unique among the trailside museums, the Norris building has a breezeway separating the two exhibit halls. The breezeway serves as a portal to the geyser basin. It is an excellent place to view the complex patterns of colorful runoff in the basin. The museum exhibits interpret geothermal geology, the basin's features, and life in geothermal areas.

Jim Peaco, National Park Service

5. Roosevelt Arch— Gateway to Wonderland

September 1903. Picture yourself stepping off a Northern Pacific Railway train after a 36-hour ride from St. Paul, Minnesota, to the dust and clamor surrounding the Gardiner depot. To the southeast, you see a 50-foot stone arch with a 30-foot-tall opening, gateway to your adventure. Your stagecoach will soon pass beneath the arch, carrying you into Yellowstone National Park.

The North Entrance was the most used entrance at that time—the year that President Theodore Roosevelt laid the cornerstone, made a speech to a throng of 2,000, and dedicated the archway that bears his name. Today, the West Entrance admits more visitors, yet Roosevelt Arch at the North Entrance remains a popular attraction.

OLD FAITHFUL INN ENDURES

What if Old Faithful Inn were not here? You might have been asking this question September 8, 1988. The previous day, a firestorm imperiled the Upper Geyser Basin, burning other structures and threatening the historic inn. Three events saved it from the inferno: a recently installed roof sprinkler system helped extinguish firebrands, the wind unexpectedly shifted away from the hotel, and well-trained, resolute firefighters stood their ground.

Jeff Henry, National Park Service

WAR PASSES THROUGH YELLOWSTONE

Imagine if you were vacationing in a war zone. That is what some hapless travelers confronted in 1877.

The traditional Nez Perce homeland encompassed 17 million acres in what is today north-central Idaho and eastern Washington and Oregon. From that, an 1855 treaty carved out a reservation of 7.5 million acres, an area more than three times the size of Yellowstone. Following the discovery of gold there, the U.S. government reduced this to 770,000 acres to accommodate white settlers. All the Nez Perce were ordered to move to the smaller reservation. Tensions rose as the army attempted to relocate the tribe.

National Park Service

Almost half of the Nez Perce tribe resisted relocation. They instead fled their homeland hoping to unite with Sitting Bull's band of Lakota in today's Alberta, Canada. Along their flight, a series of battles ensued with the U.S. Army, including skirmishes at White Bird Canyon, Cottonwood, and Clearwater in Idaho and the Big Hole, Camas Meadows, Canyon Creek, and the Bear Paw Mountains in Montana.

Between Camas Meadows and the Battle of Canyon Creek, 800 Nez Perce passed through the park from west to east, fleeing an army of 1,000 soldiers, civilian volunteers, and Indian scouts. Frustrated that they could not locate the prehistoric Bannock Trail that would lead them across the park, the Nez Perce captured an ex-prospector near the Lower Geyser Basin and forced him to guide them through the wilderness. They soon happened upon the 11-member Cowen tourist party and took them hostage. After much ordeal, all escaped. Members of a 10-person group from Helena were not as fortunate. Two were killed, while the rest escaped. Warrior groups began to range widely, harassing tourists. Within 10 days, the Nez Perce left the park and the army pursued them. Peace returned to the park.

Find the interpretive wayside relating this event at the crossing of the Grand Loop Road over Nez Perce Creek, 1 mile north of the Lower Geyser Basin. Outside of Yellowstone, the Nez Perce National Historical Park, consisting of 38 sites in Idaho, Montana, Oregon, and Washington, explores the history and culture of the Nez Perce people—and the war that bears their name.

AFTER THE BATTLE OF THE BEAR PAW

Stephanie Martin, National Park Service

"From where the sun now stands, I will fight no more forever." Chief Joseph spoke these anguished words upon his surrender to Colonel Nelson Miles, ending the Battle of the Bear Paw Mountains less than 50 miles from safe refuge in Canada. Miles promised that Joseph and his people could return to their homeland. Instead, the Nez Perce were sent to Oklahoma where they endured eight years of hardship before being allowed to return home.

But there's more to the story. During the six-day battle, Chief White Bird was able to slip away unnoticed with about 100 Nez Perce, including many children. White Bird's band eventually made it to Fort Walsh, Saskatchewan, where they joined Sitting Bull and a large band of Lakota. Some lived the rest of their days in Canada among the Piegan near Pincher Creek, Alberta.

PEOPLE ASSOCIATED WITH YELLOWSTONE

ULYSSES S. GRANT

On March 1, 1872, President Ulysses S. Grant signed An Act to Set Apart a Certain Tract of Land Lying Near the Headwaters of the Yellowstone River as a Public Park. *The park was not given a name in the statute. Today, the legislation is known as the Yellowstone Park Act.*

While visiting the park, you will encounter the names of several people who influenced the public's understanding of the region. These are the most notable explorers, surveyors, vigilantes, Native Americans, politicians, writers, photographers, and businessmen who contributed to the Yellowstone National Park story.

John Colter (1774-1813)

Believed to be the first Euro-American to travel through the Yellowstone area, his stories of an 1807-1808 winter odyssey encouraged adventurers and trappers to venture into the region. Other mountain men dubbed the hot springs and steam vents that Colter described as "Colter's Hell."

Jim Bridger (1804-1881)

Bridger was a mountain man, trapper, army guide, and explorer. It is believed that he was the first white man to see the Great Salt Lake, and in 1830 he traveled through the Yellowstone region. A lover of tall tales, Bridger inflamed people's interest in the area with stories like seeing a "peetrified forest" in which there were "peetrified birds" singing "peetrified songs." Seeing the petrified trees near Tower Junction may have inspired this story.

National Park Service

Lucius Quintus Cincinnatus Lamar (1825-1893)

The Lamar Valley is named for this Secretary of the Interior who reluctantly but wisely requested that the U.S. Army protect Yellowstone in 1885.

National Park Service

Henry D. Washburn (1832-1871)

Mount Washburn is named for this leader of an early expedition into the Yellowstone region. As the surveyor-general of Montana Territory, he led the Washburn-Langford-Doane Expedition of 1870 to explore the truths surrounding the fantastic stories about the area's geology.

W. H. Jackson, U.S. Geological Survey

Nathaniel Pitt Langford (1832-1911)

Langford's place in Montana history is well documented in his 1890 book *Vigilante Days and Ways.* The book chronicles the lawlessness around the gold fields of Virginia City and Bannack in Montana

Territory and how frontier justice was imposed. Langford was a businessman and an explorer who accompanied Washburn's 1870 expedition and became Yellowstone's first superintendent.

National Park Service

W. H. Jackson, U.S. Geological Survey

Ferdinand V. Hayden (1829-1887)

Hayden was an army surgeon and geologist who led the first government-funded surveying expedition into the Yellowstone region in 1871. His team members included photographer William Henry Jackson and painter Thomas Moran.

Thomas Moran (1837-1926)

An established artist, Moran accompanied Hayden on his survey in order to capture the colorful area on canvas. His dramatic images painted in watercolor and oil were made into prints and widely published. They helped convince Congress to protect the landscape of the upper Yellowstone River.

National Park Service

William Henry Jackson (1843-1942)

Famed as a Civil War photographer, Jackson was a member of Hayden's expedition. His images of the wonders of the Yellowstone region, along with Moran's watercolor paintings and Hayden's 500-page report, were influential in convincing Congress to set aside the lands as a park.

National Park Service

23

National Park Service

Chief Joseph (1840-1904)

Joseph was the leader of a band of the Nez Perce tribe who in 1877 fled with 800 others through Yellowstone National Park ahead of U.S. Army troops who were attempting to force them onto a reservation.

Senator George Vest (1830-1904)

National Park Service

Vest considered himself the self-appointed champion of Yellowstone. Soon after President Grant signed the act establishing the park in 1872, Vest attached an amendment to an appropriations bill that allowed the Secretary of the Interior to call upon the Secretary of War to administer the park. Vest was a Missouri defense attorney who once orated a eulogy in behalf of a dog, Old Drum, coining the phrase "man's best friend."

Theodore Roosevelt (1858-1919)

A fervent enthusiast of public lands, who, as president from 1901 to 1909, signed legislation to establish six national parks, Roosevelt had a passion for Yellowstone. While on holiday in Yellowstone in 1903, Roosevelt was invited to lay the cornerstone for the entranceway under construction at Gardiner. The feature has since been known as the Roosevelt Arch.

National Park Service

National Park Service

Stephen Mather (1867-1930)

A multi-millionaire businessman who built his fortune in the borax industry, Mather had a deep belief in the value of national parks for building better citizens. He called the parks "vast schoolrooms of Americanism." Disgusted at the deplorable conditions of the national parks in the early 1900s, Mather complained to his longtime friend, Secretary of the Interior Franklin Lane. Frustrated as well, Lane told Mather if he didn't like the way that the parks were being run he should come to Washington, D.C., and run them himself. Mather said yes, and in 1916 he became the first director of the National Park Service. Upon his death, bronze plaques were placed in every park with the words: "There will never come an end to the good that he has done." You will find Yellowstone's plaque on the trail west of the Madison Trailside Museum.

Horace Albright (1890-1987)

Albright was the protégé of Stephen Mather and served as the second superintendent of Yellowstone National Park from 1919 to 1929 and also as the second director of the National Park Service from 1929 to 1933. Under his guidance, park facilities were adapted to better serve visitors who arrived by automobile. Albright also established interpretation services. His efforts were crucial in establishing Grand Teton National Park. The Albright

National Park Service

Visitor Center in Mammoth honors his contributions.

BEST SCENIC DRIVES

There are five major entrance roads into Yellowstone, each leading to the lower or upper sections of the Grand Loop Road. Today, the highest numbers of visitors enter from West Yellowstone, followed by the South Entrance, the North Entrance at Gardiner, the East Entrance through Cody, and finally the Northeast Entrance near Cooke City.

If you have only one day to tour Yellowstone, follow the Lower Grand Loop Road to see the most accessible iconic features. For two days in the park, add the Upper Grand Loop Road to your itinerary. On a three-day vacation, you will have time to experience both Upper and Lower Grand Loop Road, and still have time to take side trips to each of the entrances. Regardless of which tour you select, plan to return and see the changes this wild Wonderland offers from year to year.

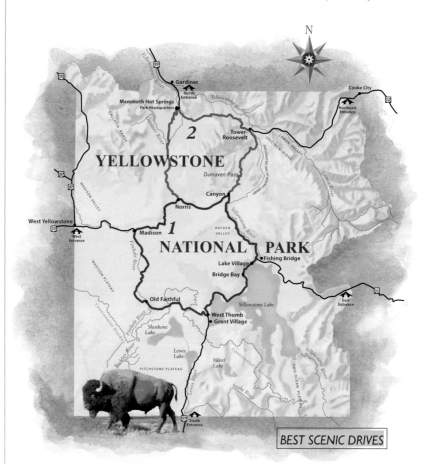

BEST SCENIC DRIVES

1. Lower Grand Loop Road

MADISON JUNCTION TO THE UPPER GEYSER BASIN

Firehole Canyon Drive
The road follows the Firehole River through a canyon and past a 40-foot waterfall. Both the canyon and waterfall are impressive. Look for golden-mantled ground squirrels at the waterfall turnout but don't feed them.

Lower Geyser Basin
Stop here to walk the boardwalk and have your first look at a geyser and mudpots. You will first pass the Fountain Paint Pots, and then the perpetual spouter, Clepsydra Geyser. The Lower Geyser Basin provides a good introduction to the curious wonders of Yellowstone.

Jim Peaco, National Park Service

Firehole Lake Drive
This one-way road is 1 mile past the Lower Geyser Basin. Here you will find Great Fountain Geyser and Firehole Lake, among other features. Great Fountain Geyser is predictable; times are often posted at the pullout. It is a marvelous geyser to photograph at sunset. A few hundred yards along the road is Firehole Lake. Expect a lot of steam to issue from its turbulent body.

Midway Geyser Basin
The unparalleled beauty of Grand Prismatic Spring is a must-see experience. You can't help but be astonished at the colorful thermophiles living in the superheated water and runoff channels. Whereas Grand Prismatic Spring seems tranquil, the Excelsior Geyser Crater that you pass along the way attests to the explosive nature of some geysers.

Biscuit Basin
The turnout for Biscuit Basin comes up fast, next to a grove of trees. The basin is famous for its colorful features, like Sapphire Pool with its odd biscuit-like deposits.

Black Sand Basin

A mile past Biscuit Basin is Black Sand Basin. Park your vehicle and walk to the viewing platform that looks across Iron Spring Creek to Cliff Geyser. This is your first opportunity for an up-close geyser experience. It is a cone geyser that erupts almost constantly, just a few feet away!

Upper Geyser Basin

Many of Yellowstone National Park's iconic features you have heard about are here: Old Faithful Geyser, Beehive Geyser, Riverside Geyser, Grotto Geyser, Grand Geyser, Castle Geyser, Giant Geyser, Morning Glory Pool, and Old Faithful Inn.

Visitor services include accommodations, restaurants, restrooms, souvenir shops, bookstores, a medical clinic, and a U.S. Post Office. Stop at the Old Faithful Visitor and Education Center for interpretive program information, predictions on when some of the geysers are expected to erupt, and trail and historic district guides.

UPPER GEYSER BASIN TO WEST THUMB

Kepler Cascades

You will find the pullout for Kepler Cascades 2.5 miles southeast of the Old Faithful overpass. Walk to the viewing platform of this 150-foot cascade that crashes through a narrow canyon of the Firehole River.

West Thumb Geyser Basin

This geyser basin is a picturesque geothermal area with outstanding panoramic views of Yellowstone Lake. Find a bench overlooking the basin and admire the sensational setting.

WEST THUMB TO CANYON VILLAGE

Gull Point Drive

If you tire of driving the Grand Loop Road, consider this leisurely alternative drive along the western shore of Yellowstone Lake. There are plenty of pullouts with short trails you can walk through the forest to the lakeshore.

Jim Peaco, National Park Service

The expansive views of the lake invite tranquility.

Lake Village

Twenty miles north of West Thumb is the intersection for Lake Village. Take the first right turn after leaving the Grand Loop Road; a sign leading to the medical clinic marks it. Drive past the clinic to the lakefront road and turn left, then park in the large lot on the lakeshore, across from the hotel. This area gives you the best views of the historic hotel and Yellowstone Lake with Stevenson Island. Visitor services include accommodations, restaurants, restrooms, souvenir shops, bookstores, a ranger station, a medical clinic, and a U.S. Post Office.

Fishing Bridge

Two miles north of Lake Village, turn onto the road to the East Entrance and Fishing Bridge. Fishing Bridge crosses the outlet of Yellowstone Lake and once was a popular spot for anglers to cast their luck for spawning trout. The

Jay Elhard, National Park Service

National Park Service determined that the trout were better left for the bears and pelicans to catch, so angling was discontinued. Walk across the bridge and look for the trout that may become meals for wildlife.

Visitor services include a campground (hard-sided units only), one of Yellowstone's trailside museums (featuring birds and a relief map of the bottom of the lake), a lunch counter, a souvenir store, a food and sundries market, and a gas station with mechanic services.

Mud Volcano

You will find the Mud Volcano pullout about 5 miles north of Fishing Bridge Junction. This is one of the most vigorous geothermal areas of the park. A short stroll on the boardwalk will convince you that Black Dragon's Cauldron and Mud Volcano are in a violently active area.

Hayden Valley

Hayden Valley begins 1 mile north of the Mud Volcano pullout. This is one of the most serene parts of the park, as the Yellowstone River courses its way through the verdant landscape. You might see herds of bison, grizzlies, wolves, bald eagles,

R. Robinson, National Park Service

sandhill cranes, and white pelicans. Winter visitors may see trumpeter swans here. There are several pullouts along the road for you to stop and admire the majesty of the valley.

South Rim Drive

You have reached two of the iconic features of the park, the Grand Canyon of the Yellowstone and the Lower Falls. Turn on to the South Rim Drive and cross the Yellowstone River over Chittenden Bridge. Make the

Jim Peaco, National Park Service

first left turn for the Upper Falls Viewpoint. After viewing the falls, proceed along South Rim Drive to the Artist Point parking area. Walk to the point. Climb the steps to the platform overlooking the sensational Grand Canyon of the Yellowstone. The wildness of the canyon seems alive with birds, geothermal steam, and the roaring cataracts of the Yellowstone River. Retrace your steps, drive back to the Grand Loop Road, and turn right for the Brink of the Upper Falls turnout.

Brink of the Upper Falls

It is a short walk down to the Yellowstone River from the parking lot. You will see Chittenden Bridge and the tumbling waters of the Yellowstone River. A few steps further and you are up close to the sheer drop of this 109-foot waterfall. Look for rainbows in the spray.

North Rim Drive

The North Rim Drive is less than 1 mile north of the Brink of the Upper Falls turnout. The one-way road terminates in Canyon Village. Before reaching the village, you will pass several short trails and viewpoints. The most impressive are the Brink of the Lower Falls, Red Rock Point, Grand View, and Inspiration Point. The Brink of the Lower Falls and Red Rock Point require short but steep descents. All four stops are worthy of your time for experiencing this amazing area packed with sensational beauty.

Canyon Junction

The North Rim Drive brings you to Canyon Village and Canyon Junction. The village has undergone extensive renovation and access redesign. Visitor services available include cabin accommodations, a campground, restaurants, restrooms, souvenir shops, bookstores, a gas station, U.S. Post Office, and the Canyon Visitor Education Center filled with revealing interpretation about geothermal activity from around the world.

CANYON JUNCTION TO NORRIS GEYSER BASIN

Virginia Cascades Drive

You will drive 10 miles before you reach the entrance to the one-way Virginia Cascades Drive. The road backtracks east 1 mile to 60-foot Virginia Cascades. Less than 0.5 mile beyond the cascades is a "Best" picnic area.

NORRIS GEYSER BASIN TO MADISON JUNCTION

Norris Geyser Basin

This is the hottest area in the park, with ground temperatures

Jim Peaco, National Park Service

approaching 190°F. Boiling water and blasting steam vents abound. Here, you will find Steamboat Geyser, the largest in the world. Its eruption is unpredictable and rare. Acquire a copy of the *Norris Geyser Basin Trail Guide* at the Norris Trailside Museum. After touring the museum, begin your exploration of Norris at Porcelain Basin. You will see geysers, steam vents, springs, pools, and beautiful thermophile micro-organisms coloring the waters.

Watch for birds known as kill-deer running over the crusted ground catching insects. Expect to see bison and elk in the spring.

Chocolate Pots

Look for dark-colored mineral-laden springs along the Gibbon River 5 miles south of Norris Junction. A small pullout on the west side of the road, just south of Gibbon River Rapids, offers the best viewing of Chocolate Pots.

Artists Paint Pots Geyser Basin
You will find this small geyser basin 6 miles south of Norris. It's a short walk from the parking area to see small geysers, fumaroles, and hot springs. The basin is noted for its colorful mudpots, from which it was given its name. Lone bull bison often stay in the area.

Gibbon Falls
Five miles north of Madison Junction is one of the most picturesque waterfalls in Yellowstone. There are several places to view this 84-foot waterfall along the Gibbon River. Cataracts like this attract American dippers. Look for them flying among the rocks and stepping into the rushing water below the falls. The Gibbon Falls Picnic Area (a "Best") is downriver from the falls.

Madison Junction
It is here that the Gibbon and Firehole Rivers join to become the Madison River. Madison Junction has a campground and one of Yellowstone's trailside museums. The museum houses an information station and Junior Ranger programming. Walk out the back of the museum toward the flagpole. A monument to Stephen Mather is placed nearby. Continue down the trail to the interpretive sign. It tells about National Park Mountain and the Washburn Expedition.

2. Upper Grand Loop Road

Mammoth to Norris Geyser Basin

Mammoth Hot Springs
Yellowstone National Park Headquarters
All of the park's administrative offices are located here, as well as a U.S. Magistrate's Office of the Department of Justice. Visit the Albright Visitor Center, where the story of the early years of Yellowstone is the theme. Walk historic Fort Yellowstone. The National Park Service offers tours of the fort during the summer season.

Visitor services at Mammoth include a campground, souvenir shops, a hotel, restaurants, U.S. Post Office, a medical clinic, gas station, and a food and sundries market.

Mammoth Hot Springs—Lower Terrace Trails

Acquire the *Mammoth Hot Springs Trail Guide* at the Albright Visitor Center. The Lower Terraces are one of the premier geothermal features in the park. You may see geysers, hot pools, and fumaroles around the park, but it is only in Mammoth that you can view travertine terraces. Iconic features include the Liberty Cap and Minerva, Mound, and Jupiter Terraces. Walk the boardwalks, but be careful: they are often slippery.

Mammoth Hot Springs—Upper Terrace Drive

The *Mammoth Hot Springs Trail Guide* is useful when touring Upper Terrace Drive. Stop at the Main Terrace Overlook to look down on Minerva, Mound, and Jupiter Terraces. When you travel the Upper Terrace Drive, look for colorful Orange Mound Spring, the unique White Elephant Back Terrace, and the last feature on the drive, Angel Terrace, which has gone through cycles of activity since Yellowstone became a park in 1872.

Swan Lake Pullout

Two miles south of Upper Terrace Drive, you pass a jumble of rocks known as the Hoodoos, and a large boulder on the canyon side of the road. You are in the area known as the Golden Gate. You will break out onto a meadow known as Gardners Hole and arrive at a pullout looking west toward Swan Lake. The view of the Gallatin Range with Electric Peak to the north and Mount Holmes to the south is superb. Trumpeter swans and other waterfowl frequent the lake. Use binoculars; avoid approaching the lake in order to not disturb the nesting birds.

Obsidian Cliff

Thirteen miles south of Mammoth is a mountain wall made of obsidian, black volcanic glass. Arrowheads and other artifacts made of this obsidian have been found hundreds of miles from this spot, suggesting that Native Americans traded the precious, strong rock.

Roaring Mountain

A large pullout 3 miles south of Obsidian Cliff provides you with good views of a hillside covered with steam vents. Geothermal activity at Roaring Mountain fluctuates, so it is always a good place to stop and note its changes.

Museum of the National Park Ranger
Turn at the sign for Norris Campground 1 mile north of Norris Junction. You will come to the historic ranger station that houses a museum just before entering the campground. The museum is dedicated to the National Park Service ranger corps. A retired ranger is often on duty during the summer season to interpret a ranger's life in the parks.

Norris Geyser Basin
See the description for the Lower Grand Loop Road.

NORRIS TO CANYON JUNCTION
See the description for Canyon Junction to Norris Geyser Basin.

CANYON JUNCTION TO MAMMOTH

Canyon Village
See the description for Canyon Junction on the West Thumb to Canyon Village.

Chittenden Road
Hiram Chittenden was the U.S. Army engineer noted for completing the Grand Loop Road system during the early 1900s. This spur road is 12 miles north of Canyon Junction. It once connected Canyon with the top of Mount Washburn and was known as the Chittenden Road. Drive the gravel road to its termination. You will be rewarded with great views of the Washburn Range to the west and the Mirror Plateau and Absaroka Range to the east.

Tower Fall
There is no "s" in the name of this 132-foot spectacle. It was decided long ago that the water fell unimpeded from Tower Creek's rock face, and therefore has a singular drop.

Tower-Roosevelt Junction
Roosevelt Lodge is located here. Yes, Teddy did camp in the area but long before the lodge was built. Visitor services include cabins, a restaurant, a food store, horseback rides, Tally-ho stagecoach rides, and Old West cookouts.

Undine Falls
A favorite waterfall with visitors, this 60-foot, three-step waterfall is 14 miles west of Tower-Roosevelt Junction (or 4 miles east of Mammoth Hot Springs).

NORTHEAST ENTRANCE TO TOWER-ROOSEVELT

Soda Butte
You will see this large, nearly dormant hot spring cone about 15 miles east of Tower-Roosevelt. It is an interesting landmark and geothermal feature where Soda Butte Creek joins the Lamar River.

J. Schmidt, National Park Service

The Lamar Valley
The river is named for Lucius Quintus Cincinnatus Lamar, a Secretary of the Interior in the late 1800s. The valley is rich in wildlife. Select any turnout along the road and look for bison, bears, wolves, coyotes, elk, raptors, and myriad waterfowl along the Lamar River.

Jim Peaco, National Park Service

BEST ROADSIDE PICNIC AREAS

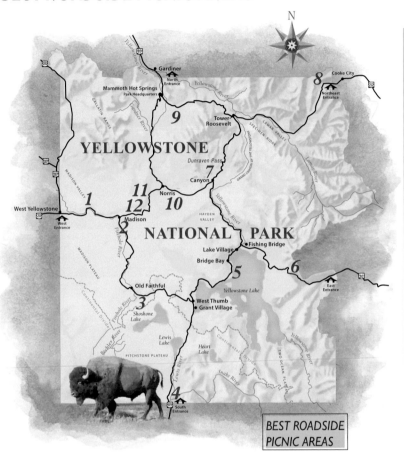

BEST ROADSIDE PICNIC AREAS

Yellowstone has 52 developed picnic areas scattered along the roadways. The following are the best for scenery and nearby activities. With the exception of Cascade Lake Trail and Gibbon Falls Picnic Areas, all of these sites have restrooms that are wheelchair accessible.

1. Madison River

The Madison River flows by the picnic grounds and under Seven-Mile Bridge along the West Entrance Road. Watch the river, fly fish, or look for wildlife in the meadows across the roadway.

2. Nez Perce

Near the confluence of Nez Perce Creek and the Firehole River, this area is adjacent to the Firehole and looks out over Fountain Flats and the Lower Geyser Basin.

3. Spring Creek

This is a lovely wooded spot about 5.5 miles southeast of the Upper Geyser Basin along the road between Old Faithful and West Thumb. The namesake creek runs directly south of the picnic area loop road.

4. Snake River

Just north of the South Entrance on the east side of the road, enjoy this forested area with picnic tables next to a side channel of the Snake River.

Ed Austin and Herb Jones, National Park Service

5. Gull Point

Gaze over Yellowstone Lake from here while enjoying your meal. There are several picnic areas around the west shore of the lake. This is the finest.

6. Sylvan Lake

This picnic area is on the north side of the road almost halfway between the East Entrance and Fishing Bridge. Additional parking pullouts on the south side of the road provide access to the shore of this

tranquil and picturesque lake. Few visitors use the picnic area, a great place to relax while enjoying a good meal.

7. Cascade Lake Trail

North of Canyon Junction, this picnic spot is a perfect place to have lunch before you "walk it off" on the short hike to Cascade Lake.

8. Warm Creek

The picnic area is in a deep forest at the Northeast Entrance. Explore the area and think about returning in the winter for cross-country skiing along the Barronette and Bannock Ski Trails.

William S. Keller, National Park Service

9. Lava Creek

Lava Creek flows out of the Blacktail Deer Plateau and under the Grand Loop Road here. The picnic area is a good place for children to play on the rocks and among the trees.

10. Virginia Cascades

You will wish you had packed a lunch when you see this picnic area near the east end of Virginia Cascades Drive just off the road between Norris and Canyon. It is in a small grove of trees next to a beautiful meadow, just after you've seen Virginia Cascades. Plan ahead, pack a lunch, and stop here.

11. Gibbon Meadows

This lovely spot is about 2 miles south of Norris on the road to Madison Junction. Nine picnic tables front the Gibbon River.

12. Gibbon Falls

You can explore the Gibbon River immediately below the waterfall from this recently constructed picnic area on the east side of the road between Madison Junction and Norris. The picnic tables are close to the river, with a lot of room to roam and explore.

BEST BICYCLE RIDES

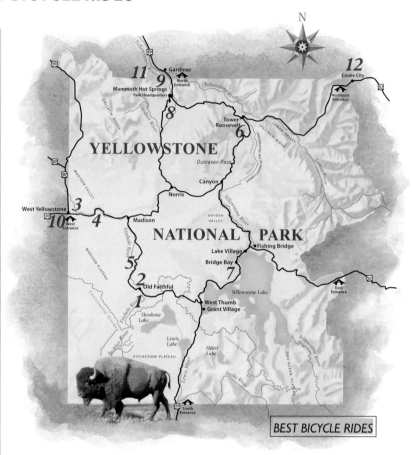

BEST BICYCLE RIDES

Yellowstone provides many opportunities for stretching your legs and viewing the park at five times the speed of walking. For experienced cyclists, much of the Grand Loop has shoulders wide enough for bicycles and motor vehicles to share the road, but heavy traffic during the busy summer season discourages most cyclists. The best rides for the casual rider are short and away from bothersome traffic.

1. Lone Star Geyser

Locate the trailhead 1 mile southeast of the Old Faithful area along the Grand Loop Road, near Kepler Cascades. The round-trip distance is 5 miles, over an abandoned roadway.

2. *Old Faithful Inn to Morning Glory Pool*

Ride at a leisurely pace past Castle Geyser, Grotto Geyser, Fan and Mortar Geysers, Riverside Geyser, and on to Morning Glory Pool. You can return, making it a 2-mile excursion, or take a side route to Biscuit Basin, adding an additional 1 mile to your ride. Didn't bring your bike? A concessionaire rents bicycles in the Snow Lodge gift shop.

Jim Peaco, National Park Service

3. *Riverside Trail*

This 1-mile one-way ride goes from near the West Entrance to the Madison River. Your destination is where the National Park Service once maintained a horse barn and corral for backcountry patrols. The facility was removed, but you can imagine why park managers selected this location. Make sure that you pack food. This is an ideal family ride, and a picnic table awaits you at the river.

4. *West Entrance Road*

This is an ideal ride in late winter and early spring when the road is bare but remains barricaded to automobiles, and the over-the-snow vehicles are no longer running. Experience the solitude of Yellowstone before the onslaught of visitors. You can ride from West Yellowstone to Seven-Mile Bridge and, if you wish, another 7 miles to Madison Junction.

5. *Fountain Freight Road*

Once called National Park Avenue, this 3.5-mile one-way gravel roadbed crosses the Lower Geyser Basin. The best way to access this ride is to drive to the end of Fountain Flat Drive south of Madison Junction and unload in the large parking area. Ride through the geyser basin to the Fairy Falls parking lot on the Grand Loop Road, then return.

6. Old Chittenden Service Road

This 2-mile (one-way) unpaved road between the Grand Loop Road and Tower Fall Campground is best suited to mountain bikes.

7. Natural Bridge Road Near Bay Bridge

Easy and level, this is a leisurely 2-mile round-trip ride for your family. Viewing the natural bridge is worth the ride.

8. Bunsen Peak Road and Golden Gate Service Road

Access this 6-mile (one-way) ride from the southeast edge of the seasonal housing complex in Mammoth Hot Springs. This is a challenging ride for anyone who has not trained or recently ridden.

National Park Service

9. Old Mammoth Road

Begin behind the Mammoth Hotel and follow the gravel road 5 miles to Gardiner. Watch for bison and pronghorn.

10. Rendezvous Ski Trails in West Yellowstone

More than 20 miles of cross-country ski trails offer ideal bicycling opportunities.

11. Old Yellowstone Trail from Gardiner

An easy out-and-back pedal on a gravel road along the Yellowstone River heads northwest from Roosevelt Arch.

12. Daisy and Lulu Passes from Cooke City

Twenty-six miles of old mining roads provide summer access to the high country of the Beartooth Plateau between Cooke City and the Absaroka-Beartooth Wilderness boundary.

BEST HORSE ACTIVITIES

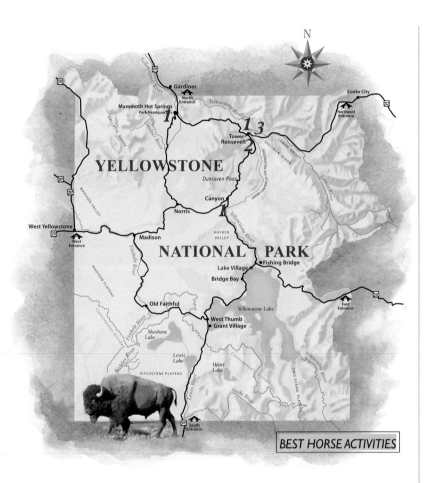

BEST HORSE ACTIVITIES

Do you want a sense of how Teddy Roosevelt traveled through Yellowstone? A horseback ride offers you a feeling of bygone adventures, riding through meadows and forests on a mild-mannered steed. Which rides are the best? It depends on your riding ability and how long you want to be in the saddle. You may also consider additional unique experiences: riding in an Old West stagecoach and attending a cookout. For information on prices and reservations, see www.yellowstonenationalparklodges. com/things-to-do/summer-things-to-do/wild-west-adventures.

Jim Peaco, National Park Service

1. Easy One- and Two-Hour Horseback Rides

Depart from Mammoth Hot Springs, Roosevelt, and Canyon. Ride though sagebrush-covered hills, and listen to the Old West stories revealed by your wrangler.

2. Ride a Stagecoach

Climb aboard a replica Tally-ho coach, similar to those used for touring the park in the late 1800s. Rides are one hour from the Roosevelt corral.

3. Go to an Old West Cookout

National Park Service

Curious about what it was like to be a cowboy long ago? Attend an Old West cookout and have dinner around a campfire, enjoy western music, listen to storytelling, and eat cowboy-style cooking. Reservations are required. Wagons leave from Roosevelt each afternoon.

Regardless of the activity you choose, all of them will help you to imagine what it was like to travel in "Wonderland" in the early days.

BEST DAY HIKES

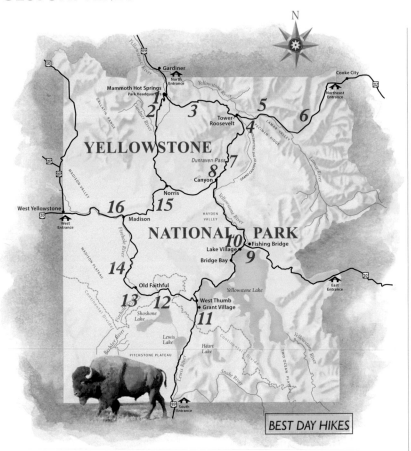

Jim Peaco, National Park Service

Driving the Grand Loop Road makes you want to experience the sights, sounds, and fragrances of Yellowstone. It's time to get out of your car and experience the park! Yellowstone is big, and it can be difficult to select the best places to take a short walk. Here are the 15 best easy-to-moderate walks (and 1 strenuous hike) covering each geographic area of Yellowstone within reach of the Grand Loop Road. The hikes take you to pristine lakes, memorable waterfalls, amazing

VISITING BEAR COUNTRY

*You might ask: "Is it safe for me to
hike in bear country?"*
*Yes, but there are always risks involved
when you are in their territory. Read and
follow all the suggestions for hiking in
bear country given out in literature by
park rangers when you enter Yellowstone. Look for updated information
posted at trailheads.*

Jim Peaco, National Park Service

"What measures should I take while hiking?"
*Avoid surprising a bear by being alert, hiking mid-day with a group, and mak-
ing noise. Make your presence known, even on trails close to development. Bears
roam the entire park. Carry bear pepper spray. Finally, don't call out phases like,
"Here bear, here bear!" to warn bears. Hikers approaching out-of-sight will hear
"BEAR!" and might react inappropriately.*

"But what if I encounter a bear on a trail?"
*There is no simple answer. Bears react differently to each situation. Here are some
suggestions from hikers who have encountered bears:*

- *Know that all bears can be dangerous.*
- *Never run! Instead, back away slowly.*
- *Talk to the bear in a soft, calm voice.*
- *Turn sideways, or bend at the knees
  to appear small.*
- *Keep an eye on the bear, but avoid
  a stare down.*
- *Detour far around the bear if you
  must go forward on the trail.*
- *If the bear charges, use pepper spray.
  If the bear attacks, protect your chest
  and abdomen by falling to the ground on
  your stomach or assuming a fetal position.*
- *Leave your backpack on. Cover the back of your neck with your hands.
  Do not move until the bear has left.*

BEAR ATTACK:
Are you Prepared to Avoid One?

BE ALERT

MAKE NOISE

CARRY BEAR SPRAY

AVOID HIKING ALONE

DO NOT RUN

- During a surprise encounter - slowly back away
- If the bear charges - stand your ground & use your bear spray
- If the bear attacks during a surprise encounter - play dead
- If the bear persistently stalks you then attacks - fight back
- If a bear attacks you in your tent – fight back

There is no guarantee of your safety in bear country

National Park Service

Remember: you are a guest in bear country; be a good one.

overlooks, or iconic geothermal areas. Get out of your car and discover! Prepare ample provisions and clothing for hiking high-altitude trails. For added enjoyment, I recommend that you take a sack lunch on all of these hikes. Carry an extra bag to pack out your litter. Keep in mind that discarded orange peels, apple cores, sunflower seed shells, and pistachio nutshells take many years to deteriorate at these elevations, plus you don't want to "feed" wildlife. Backcountry rangers have seen an increase in these unsightly leavings along the trails and at picnic spots. Enjoy the backcountry, and help keep Yellowstone as pristine as you found it.

1. Beaver Ponds Loop

Level of difficulty: Moderate

Duration: 3 hours

Distance: 5-mile loop

Elevation change: 400 feet in 0.5 mile, then gentle

Best time of the year: Anytime when the trail is free of snow

J. Schmidt, National Park Service

Trailhead: Begin on Beaver Ponds Trail located by the stone house and the parking lot on the north side of Clematis Creek north of the Liberty Cap. Trailhead signs are labeled for Sepulcher Mountain and Beaver Ponds.

Special note: Beaver are most active in the evenings, through the night, and during early morning. You will see many waterfowl if you arrive at the ponds at mid-day. Bring your binoculars.

The hike: The trail offers a gentle climb through mixed forests and meadows to the ponds. The soft sounds of Clematis Creek play to your left. Continue walking straight when you encounter the Sepulcher Mountain Trail on the left. Your trail leads though grassy meadows and forested areas until you pass three ponds. After your exploration, follow the trail onto a sagebrush plateau and the gravel Old Gardiner Road. Watch for pronghorn and raptors as you follow the road back to the Mammoth Hotel, a short distance from where you began the hike.

2. Snow Pass –
Hoodoos Loop
Level of difficulty:
Moderate
Duration: 4+ hours
Distance: 6.2-mile loop
Elevation change:
640 feet
Best time of the year:
Mid-June through September

RG Johnsson, National Park Service

Trailhead: The trail leaves from the Glen Creek Trailhead, 5 miles south of Mammoth Hot Springs on the Mammoth-Norris Road. Park on the east side of the road at the Bunsen Peak Trailhead and walk across the road to the trail heading northwest by the creek. This is often a busy parking lot.

Special note: Black bears and grizzly bears frequent the Snow Pass area. Visitors like seeing bears. Some people want to see them from the trail rather than from their vehicle. When I was a ranger-naturalist at Mammoth Hot Springs, I was assigned to lead a weekly "bear hike" through Snow Pass. We frequently observed bears. Read Visiting Bear Country on page 45.

The hike: This hike circumnavigates 8,000-foot Terrace Mountain. Along the way, you will pass along Glen Creek as it flows through open meadows. You will also enter mixed forests of aspen, spruce, and fir, climb over 7,450-feet Snow Pass, and walk through a jumble of ancient travertine called the Hoodoos.

Like most trails in Yellowstone, this route is easy to follow. Just be aware of needing to make decisions at trail junctions. The first decision is shortly after your hike begins. Turn right to follow the Howard Eaton Trail and walk past an area of yellow rock called the Golden Gate, and then through the Hoodoos. Continue 2.5 miles along the base of Terrace Mountain to the Snow Pass trail leading west. The trail is a moderate climb. Snow Pass was a stagecoach route before the Grand Loop Road was constructed through the Golden Gate.

Walk over Snow Pass and arrive at the Glen Creek Trail. You will find two other trails in the area which lead to Sportsman Lake and Sepulcher Mountain. Turn left and hike south 2 miles along Glen Creek back to the trailhead.

3. Wraith Falls

Level of difficulty: Easy

Duration: 1 hour

Distance: 1 mile round-trip

Elevation change: Minimal

Best time of the year: Anytime after the snows have melted on the trail and before late August when water flow diminishes.

Trailhead: The Wraith Falls Trailhead is 0.5 mile east of the Lava Creek Picnic Area along the Grand Loop Road.

Special note: The 80-foot cascade provides excellent habitat for American dippers, a water-loving bird.

John H. Boyd

The hike: Follow the well-traveled pathway to the overlook. You will pass through sagebrush, meadows, some marshy areas, and forests on your walk.

The water from Lupine Creek tumbles down a rock face, making Wraith Falls a cascade rather than a true waterfall. Its appearance led to its name, which means a mental representation of some haunting experience—a phantom or a ghost. You'll see why.

4. Yellowstone River Picnic Area to Bannock Ford Overlook

Level of difficulty: Moderate

Duration: 2 hours

Distance: 3.7-mile loop

Elevation change: 200 feet in the first 0.5 mile, then level

National Park Service.

Best time of the year: Early spring and autumn. Summer is too hot.

Trailhead: Access the trail at the Yellowstone River Picnic Area, 1.25 miles east of Tower-Roosevelt Junction, along the Northeast Entrance Road.

Special note: Spring is the best time of year to enjoy the profusion of wildflowers blooming in the area. Look for bighorn sheep along the steep cliffs. The trail terminates at a promontory with a view of the confluences of Tower and Antelope Creeks with the Yellowstone River. This area is significant as the only place where the Yellowstone River can be crossed on foot, known as the Bannock Ford. Native Americans crossed here to and from the buffalo grounds on the plains of Montana and Wyoming.

The hike: This hike takes you close to the geologic wonders of lower Yellowstone Canyon. While walking over sage-covered hills and skirting Douglas-fir groves, you will encounter glacial boulders deposited erratically 12,000 years ago. Gaze northeast to the Beartooth Plateau where these boulders originated. The canyon itself is fascinating, with tall spires, colorful walls, and overhanging cliffs. Look around when you reach the promontory. The vast Absaroka Range stands to the east, with the Washburn Range to the south. Below is Bannock Ford—imagine wading across the river's strong current!

You can retrace your steps to the trailhead, or choose to extend your walk and make a loop. If so, continue to the next trail junction, turn left onto the Specimen Ridge Trail, and descend to the road. This requires that you walk along the roadway 0.7 mile back to the trailhead.

5. Slough Creek

Level of difficulty: Moderate
Duration: 5 hours
Distance: 7 miles round-trip
Elevation change: 400 feet
Best time of the year: June through October; autumn is very good for fall colors.
Trailhead: From the junction at Tower-Roosevelt, drive 6 miles east on the Northeast Entrance Road to the signed turnoff for Slough Creek Campground on the left. Follow the gravel road almost 2 miles to the trailhead on the right.

Special note: Bears frequent this area, particularly in the spring. The trail follows an old wagon road to the historic Silver Tip Ranch. The road is the only access to the ranch. You might encounter horse-drawn

Jim Peaco, National Park Service

wagons during your hike. The trail follows Slough Creek. Give yourself plenty of time to break away from the trail to investigate the lively creek.

The hike: Your destination is the second large meadow along Slough Creek. Follow the wagon road through patchy Douglas-fir forests and aspen groves for 2 miles to the first meadow. You know that you have arrived at the meadow when you see the Buffalo Plateau Trail breaking off to the left, and you glimpse the Slough Creek backcountry patrol cabin tucked among the trees. Continue on the Slough Creek Trail another 1.5 miles to the second meadow. During summer, you will enjoy wonderful wildflower displays in both meadows. The boulders strewn about are granite basement rocks formed more than 2.5 million years ago and moved here from the Beartooth Plateau during successive ice age events. Return to the trailhead by retracing your steps.

6. Trout Lake

Level of difficulty: Easy
Duration: 1 to 2 hours
Distance: 1.2 miles round-trip
Elevation change: 150 feet
Best time of the year: Springtime to see the trout spawning, summer and autumn for the sheer beauty of the area.
Trailhead: Watch for the small parking area about 1.5 miles south of Pebble Creek Campground, along the Northeast Entrance Road.

Special note: Your initial reaction to the direction you will be hiking may not impress you. Go for it anyway; the splendor of the lake and its setting is worth your time.

The hike: The trail climbs a steep ridge through an Engelmann spruce and

Ed Fuhr Photography

Douglas-fir forest. From the top of the hill, the lake appears below. Once you reach the 12-acre lake, walk all the way around it. The views from all angles are wonderful. The inlet stream on the north end is where you'll find cutthroat trout spawning during spring. Bears know this, too, so be alert.

7. Mount Washburn

Level of difficulty: Strenuous
Duration: 4 hours
Distance: 6.2 miles round-trip
Elevation change: 1,400 feet
Best time of the year: Late June through September
Trailhead: Dunraven Pass Trailhead, 5 miles north of Canyon Junction on the road to Tower Fall. The trail begins from the top of the pass. The parking area is often crowded. If the lot at Dunraven Pass is full, drive 5 miles north to the gravel Chittenden Road on the east side of the road. Turn right and drive 1.4 miles south to the parking lot and trailhead for the summit. From here, hike 3 miles on the old roadbed to the summit.

Special note: You will hike through exposed alpine meadows. Bring ample

Ed Austin and Herb Jones, National Park Service

water and wear sun protection. The weather can change quickly and with little warning. You could experience sleet and snow, even in the middle of summer. Bring a jacket just in case.

The hike: This is a premier hike. The profusion of wildflowers and expansive views are unparalleled in Yellowstone. Plan additional time to photograph and explore.

The trail is popular, well worn (following an old road), and easy to follow. Your destination is the summit lookout at 10,243 feet. It will be in view before the last mile.

Longtime park naturalist Bill Lewis relates a story in his book *Moose Droppings* about a ranger-led hike he was conducting on this trail. He told the group that it was common to see moose on Mount Washburn. A visitor disagreed, declaring that moose live only in marshy areas. Bill did not argue. They rounded the second switchback and came face-to-face with two moose: a cow and her calf. Seeing is believing.

RG Johnsson, National Park Service

8. Cascade Lake

Level of difficulty: Easy
Duration: 2 to 3 hours
Distance: 5 miles round-trip
Elevation change: Minimal
Best time of the year: June through October
Trailhead: There are two trailheads available. One is along the Canyon-Norris Road, and the other is on the Grand Loop Road. I encourage you to use the latter trailhead, located in a picnic area 1.25 miles north of Canyon Junction on the road toward Dunraven Pass.

Special note: Hiking to Cascade Lake in the early summer will reward you with a profusion of wildflowers blooming in the meadows. Several of the iconic species you will encounter are identified in this book.

The hike: Follow the well-marked trail at the west side of the picnic area. Continue about 1 mile until you arrive at the Cascade Lake Trail. Continue to the right for another mile to the lake.

The trail starts in an old lodgepole pine forest and winds through areas burned during the fires of 1988. Notice the mosaic burn pattern. High winds forced firebrands to jump over some groves, landing in others. After a mile, you will arrive at Cascade Creek and follow it the remainder of the way to the lake as it passes through forests and meadows. Expansive meadows west and north of the lake afford views to the summit of 9,397-foot Observation Peak and the ridge connecting to Dunraven Pass.

9. Storm Point

Level of difficulty: Easy
Duration: 2 hours
Distance: 2.3-mile loop
Elevation change: Minimal
Best time of the year: All summer
Trailhead: The trail leaves from the large parking area at Indian Pond turnout, 3 miles east of Fishing Bridge on the south side of the East Entrance Road.

Special note: Yellow-bellied marmots inhabit the often windy point. You will see that marmots live in some of the most difficult and beautiful landscapes in Yellowstone.

The hike: The trail starts as a single path then splits to become a loop. Go clockwise or counterclockwise, it's your choice. The Storm Point Trail runs almost flat, leading you first through sagebrush meadows with a few large lodgepole pines and then, if you are hiking clockwise, a spruce-fir forest. The view from the point is 220 degrees of Yellowstone Lake grandeur. The section of trail that parallels the shore traverses lake dunes that reach several hundred yards inland, attesting to the centuries of heavy wind action at Storm Point. After reaching the point, the loop trail leads back into the woods, this time through a mixed-age lodgepole pine forest, interspersed with whitebark pines and Engelmann spruce.

10. Elephant Back Mountain

Level of difficulty: Moderate
Duration: 2 hours
Distance: 4-mile loop
Elevation change: 800 feet
Best time of the year: Mid-June through September
Trailhead: From Fishing Bridge Junction, drive 1 mile south on the road toward Lake Village. Watch for the signed trailhead pullout on the west side of the road.

Special note: Elephant Back Mountain is a 70,000-year-old lava flow, recent for Yellowstone's geologic clock. Views of Yellowstone Lake, the Absaroka Range, and Lake Hotel are outstanding. You will find several places to sit at the summit. Pack a lunch and linger.

Richard Lake, National Park Service

The hike: The first leg of the trail briefly parallels the road, then veers into the trees. After 1 mile at a generally easy grade, the trail splits to become a loop. Select the left fork because the switchbacks are easier to hike up than those on the right.

The trail travels through an old lodgepole pine forest that did not succumb to the fires of 1988. The forest is progressing, with shade-tolerant spruce trees and firs growing beneath taller lodgepole pines. You will reach the top after six switchback turns. Your return trip includes another six switchbacks that are a bit steeper.

11. Riddle Lake

Level of difficulty: Easy

Duration: 3 hours

Distance: 5 miles round-trip

Elevation change: Minimal

Best time of the year: Mid-July to October

RG Johnsson, National Park Service

Trailhead: You will find the well-marked trailhead 3 miles south of Grant Village junction on the South Entrance Road, near the Continental Divide sign.

Special note: As part of Yellowstone's bear management program, this trail is closed in the spring and opens about July 15. However, bears can be in this area anytime during the visitor season. Get updated information from a visitor center or ranger station before taking this walk.

The hike: The trail is a level walk that crosses the Continental Divide. There are no other trails in the area to confuse you.

Follow the trail through the woods, along streams, and across flower-blanketed meadows to this peaceful lake. Along the way, you will see several of the flowers discussed in this book: heartleaf arnica, shooting star, and monkshood. You may also happen upon one of the iconic animals of Yellowstone. Moose favor the marshy areas through which you are walking, and the wetlands around this 275-acre lake.

12. DeLacy Creek to Shoshone Lake

Level of difficulty: Easy

Duration: 4 hours

Distance: 6 miles round-trip

Elevation change: Minimal

Best time of the year: Mid-June through September

RG Johnsson, National Park Service

Trailhead: On the Old Faithful-West Thumb Road, look for the trailhead sign at DeLacy Creek, 9 miles east of the Old Faithful overpass or 9 miles west of West Thumb Junction. A pullout for parking is on the north side of the road about 200 yards west of the DeLacy Creek Picnic Area. The trail begins on the south side of the road just west of the parking area.

Special note: Moose, elk, mule deer, black bears, and sandhill cranes are sometimes seen along the route. Shoshone Lake is the largest freshwater lake in the lower 48 states that can be reached only by canoe or foot.

The hike: Look and listen both ways before crossing the Old Faithful-West Thumb Road to the trailhead—the bend in the road makes it difficult to see oncoming traffic. The trail drops into the DeLacy Creek drainage, then descends more gradually 3 miles to the north shore of Shoshone Lake.

The trail follows DeLacy Creek on an easy grade, at first traveling through lodgepole pine forests, then skirting riparian meadows.

You will know you are getting close to the lake when the trail reenters the forest. There is plenty of driftwood scattered about the lakeshore, offering good seating and places to picnic.

R. Robinson, National Park Service

13. Lone Star Geyser

Level of difficulty: Easy
Duration: 3 hours
Distance: 4.8 miles round-trip
Elevation change: Minimal
Best time of the year: Summer to early fall

Trailhead: Look for the trailhead 3.5 miles southeast of the Old Faithful overpass on the west side of the road. The trailhead leaves just south of the Kepler Cascades pullout.

Special note: This trail follows an old, partially paved road and is also a bicycle pathway. Stay alert for traffic approaching from behind. Check with the Old Faithful Visitor Education Center before you begin your hike for reports of when the geyser last erupted. As one of the more regular geysers in the park, it erupts about every three hours.

The hike: The trail is well marked and popular, though never crowded. It leads south from the trailhead, crosses a bridge at 0.75 mile over the Firehole River, and ends at the massive 12-foot-tall geyser cone.

Your hike takes you along the Firehole River and through a lodgepole pine and spruce-fir forest that the 1988 fires missed. High winds blew firebrands over the valley, saving it from the firestorm. The first 2 miles of your walk are along the old West Thumb-Old Faithful stagecoach road. At 2 miles, you reach the confluence of Spring Creek and the Firehole River. The stagecoach road followed Spring Creek east. You will continue south on the road that the U.S. Army cut in 1895 to access Lone Star Geyser.

Cross the wooden bridge over the geyser's runoff channels and find a comfortable spot in the viewing area to wait for the next eruption. Check the log book to see if anyone recorded the time of the previous eruption. If you packed a picnic lunch, enjoy your meal while Lone Star gurgles and splashes before finally spouting a fine stream 45 feet high.

14. Fairy Falls

Level of difficulty: Easy
Duration: 4 hours
Distance: 8 miles round-trip
Elevation change: 200 feet
Best time of the year: The trail opens in late May and stays open through October in most years. Go early in the season when spring runoff is at its height. Or, see the waterfall during the hot summer months and sit near the pool to enjoy the refreshing spray. Much of the trail lacks shade, so wear a hat and bring plenty of drinking water.

Trailhead: There are two access points to Fairy Falls. This description follows the longer route because the parking lot and trail are less crowded.

Kurt Johnson, Wild Things of Wyoming

Turn onto Fountain Flat Drive, 2 miles north of the Lower Geyser Basin. Drive to the end of the road and park in the large lot. (To shave 1.5 miles round-trip off the hike, park at the busier trailhead lot 1 mile south of Midway Geyser Basin, cross the steel bridge, and hike Fountain Freight Road 1 mile to the Fairy Lake Trailhead.)

Special note: For further adventure, continue another 0.6 mile to Spray and Imperial Geysers.

The hike: The first part of your hike is along an abandoned roadbed that once served as a freight road for the concessions in the geyser basins. Today hikers, bicyclists, and cross-country skiers have exclusive use of the road. After 1.75 miles, you will reach the trail sign for Fairy Falls. Hike 1.6 miles west to reach the falls. The trail follows along the edge of the Madison Plateau, a giant lava flow of 640,000 years ago. You will notice that change is constant in this area as you walk through a lodgepole pine forest regenerating after the 1988 fire.

Continuing along the trail, you will soon hear crashing water from Fairy Creek as it splashes into a pool 197 feet below the Madison Plateau. Fairy Falls is exquisite.

15. Artists Paint Pots

Level of difficulty: Easy
Duration: 1 hour
Distance: 1-mile loop
Elevation change: 100 feet
Best time of the year: Summer
Trailhead: The signed parking area and trailhead are 3.8 miles south of Norris Junction.
Special note: The paint pots can fling hot mud surprisingly far. Avoid being splattered.
The hike: The trail begins on a boardwalk, then becomes a pathway until it reaches the geothermal area. The trail splits; walk to your left around the paint pots and up Paint Pot Hill. Return to the parking lot by completing the loop trail.

The beginning of the hike is through a lodgepole pine forest that burned in 1988. Notice the thick "doghair" growth of the new trees. You also pass meadows with dead, standing lodgepole pines that did not burn. Instead, they were killed by the ever-changing distribution of water in the area. Silica-laden water invaded their water source, killing the trees. Notice the white bands on the lower reaches of the trunks. You are looking at silica that was absorbed by the trees. Known as "bobbysocks trees," you will see dozens of them east of the Lower Geyser Basin along the Grand Loop Road.

Jim Peaco, National Park Service

The trail then takes you to a small geyser basin that has every geothermal feature that Yellowstone has to offer. You will first encounter two small geysers near the trail. Both are recognized as perpetual spouters because they never stop erupting. As you walk up Paint Pot Hill, you will see hissing fumaroles, colorful mudpots, and beautiful steaming pools. After taking a lot of photographs, complete the loop to return to the parking lot.

16. Harlequin Lake
Level of difficulty: Easy
Duration: 1 hour
Distance: 1 mile round-trip
Elevation change: Minimal
Best time of the year: Anytime
Trailhead: The trailhead is located 1.5 miles west of Madison Junction along the West Entrance Road. Park in the lot on the south side of the road. The trail leaves from the east end of the parking lot on the north side of the road.

J. Schmidt, National Park Service

Special note: The area around the lake burned during the 1988 fires. You can return each year to observe forest succession.

The hike: This gentle trail begins in an open meadow across from the Madison River and soon enters a young lodgepole pine forest. After a short stroll through this forest, you reach the lake. Waterfowl frequent the lake, but not harlequin ducks (they prefer fast-moving streams).

BEST SELF-GUIDED TRAIL GUIDES

Jim Peaco, National Park Service

Area trail guides are available at all visitor centers. The guides include trail maps and natural and cultural heritage information. I recommend that you acquire all of these. For a small donation, they will enhance your Yellowstone experience.

Old Faithful Historic District: A Brief History & Walking Tour
Curious about how this area looked in bygone times? Do you want to know some details about Old Faithful Inn? This walking tour will provide you with insights into one of the most iconic areas in the National Park System.

Old Faithful Area Trail Guide
The Upper Geyser Basin appears overwhelming upon first sight. It's large, with dozens of geysers and hot springs. Are you looking for the famed Morning Glory Pool or renowned Grand Geyser? The trail guide is an excellent resource for locating the many geothermal features in this part of the Upper Geyser Basin and includes Biscuit Basin and Black Sand Basin.

Norris Geyser Basin Trail Guide:
Including Porcelain and Back Basins
The guide is a walking tour of the hottest land area in the United States. Use the guide to help you read the temperatures of the waters by observation. There are two geyser basins at Norris: Porcelain Basin and Back Basin. The pamphlet is essential for appreciating the geothermal features within.

Mammoth Hot Springs Trail Guide:
Including Lower Terraces and Upper Terrace Drive
The pamphlet will help you understand how superheated water dissolves ancient seabed deposits to sculpt this unique geothermal feature. The Upper Terrace Drive is a popular ski trail in winter.

West Thumb Geyser Basin Trail Guide:
Including Fishing Cone and Thumb Paint Pots
The trail guide describes the geology of the geyser basin, a brief history of the site, and a map that will help you find Twin Geysers, Abyss Pool, Black Pool, and Fishing Cone.

Canyon Area Trail Guide:
Featuring the Grand Canyon of the Yellowstone River,
Including North Rim Drive and South Rim Drive
Getting the most from your time at Canyon can be challenging if you don't have a plan. This trail guide will help you decide what interests you most.

All of these guides are made available by private funding from either the Yellowstone Association or the Yellowstone Park Foundation, in cooperation with the National Park Service.

BEST BACKPACKING

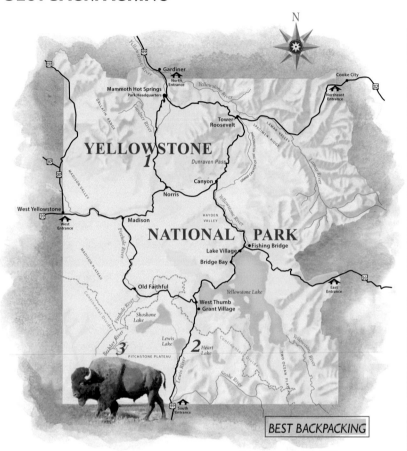

BEST BACKPACKING

Ninety-seven percent of Yellowstone National Park is wilderness, accessible only by watercraft, horseback, or foot. You can see much of the park from vistas along the Grand Loop and entrance roads. To get a feeling for the vastness of 2.2 million acres of wildness, however, you will want to get away from the crowds. A night in the backcountry provides you the opportunity to experience nature on an intimate level.

Backcountry camping requires a permit. Review Backcountry Camping & Hiking and Online Backcountry Trip Planner for details at nps.gov/yell/planyourvisit/backcountryhiking.htm.

The following are descriptions of three of the park's best overnight hikes that will introduce you to Yellowstone's backcountry.

I. *Grizzly Lake*

Level of difficulty: Moderate

Duration: Overnight

Distance: 7 miles one way

Elevation change: 800 feet

Best time of the year: Mid-June through October

RG Johnsson, National Park Service

Trailhead: The trailhead to Grizzly Lake is located on the road between Mammoth Hot Springs and Norris, about 15 miles south of Mammoth or 6 miles north of Norris. Watch for the signed trailhead at a pullout on the west side of the road, about 1 mile south of Beaver Lake.

Special note: You can do this hike either as a 6-mile out-and-back from the Grizzly Lake Trailhead, or as a 7-mile through-hike with a short vehicle shuttle between the Grizzly Lake and Mount Holmes Trailheads on the road between Mammoth and Norris. Either way, much of the route passes through lush regrowth of lodgepole pines after the 1988 fires. Due to the dense vegetation, be sure to follow Visiting Bear Country guidelines (see page 45).

The hike: The trail heads north with a bridge over Obsidian Creek. Turn left at the junction with the Howard Eaton Trail. You will soon meet some switchbacks that climb a ridge with good views of 1.5-mile-long Grizzly Lake and 10,336-foot Mount Holmes. Study the lake and look for places to explore after you set up camp. In the next mile, the trail drops to the lake. Stay to the right around the northern end of the lake. Continue north along Straight Creek to the campsite. If it's available, request Campsite 1C1 when you obtain your backcountry permit. At the far southern end of the lake, Straight Creek supplies most of the water to the 36-foot-deep lake and provides excellent spawning habitat for brook trout.

When you leave, you can simply retrace your steps on the Grizzly Lake Trail. Or, for fresh scenery, follow Straight Creek north, cross Winter Creek, and go to the right at the junction with the Mount Holmes Trail. The trail arcs to the right and again crosses Winter Creek. Soon you will parallel the Grand Loop Road. Your hike ends at the Mount Holmes Trailhead. Shuttle your vehicle to the Grizzly Lake Trailhead 3 miles south.

2. Heart Lake

Level of difficulty:
Moderate
Duration: 2 to 3 days
Distance: 16 miles round-
trip
Elevation change: 500 feet
Best time of the year:
July to September
Trailhead: The Heart

RG Johnsson, National Park Service

Lake Trail begins 6 miles south of Grant Village Junction and just
north of Lewis Lake off the South Entrance Road.

Special note: The bear management area surrounding Heart Lake is
closed to hikers from April 1 through June 30. This is bear and moose
country. Make your presence known.

There are several campsites from which to choose around Heart
Lake. Consult with the backcountry ranger's desk about your options.

The hike: The well-maintained Heart Lake Trail traverses one of
the more pristine areas in Yellowstone. The first section of the trail
climbs very gradually across a ravine and through a partially burned
forest. At 5.5 miles, you reach a ridge. You are standing at 8,140 feet
and can see Heart Lake below. The view is one of the most beautiful
sights in the park. From here, the trail loses 200 feet in elevation over
2.5 miles to the Witch Creek drainage and Heart Lake Geyser Basin.
Heart Lake Geyser Basin comprises five groups of fumaroles, springs,
and 19 geysers, many of them perpetual spouters. The Rustic group
is the most active, with Rustic Geyser bursting to 50 feet on regular
intervals. This group is 0.5 mile south of the Heart Lake Ranger Station
and about 1,000 feet west of the lake.

Skirt the bright blue geothermal pools that dot the meadow on the
left-hand side of the trail. After passing the pools, follow a creek for a
short distance and cross the valley until you see the Heart Lake Ranger
Station, about 100 yards from the lake. The trail reaches the shore
of Heart Lake at mile 7.4 and travels west for the final 0.5 mile to 10
backcountry campsites.

Watch for several species of birds along the lake's shore; the rare
trumpeter swan nests here. You may see a wide variety of wildlife around

the lake. The Heart Lake area is home to moose, deer, pikas, elk, trumpeter swans, grizzly bears, and wolves.

Mount Sheridan rises west of the lake. With binoculars, you can see a small hut on top of this 10,400-foot mountain. To the east is Chicken Ridge and the Absaroka Range. Reserve your campsite for two nights to allow a day for exploring the area. On the final day, retrace your route to return to the trailhead.

3. Bechler River to Old Faithful

Diane Renkin, National Park Service

Level of difficulty: Moderate

Duration: 3 days, 2 nights

Distance: 28 miles one way

Elevation change: 1,600 feet

Best time of the year: Late July to September.

Trailhead: From Idaho Falls, Idaho, drive 53 miles north on U.S. Highway 20 to Ashton, Idaho. Turn right onto Main Street, which is also Idaho Highway 47. Drive east about 6 miles on Idaho 47, turn right on Green Timber Road, and continue east. After 5.5 miles, the pavement ends. Drive east on the dirt road, now designated Cave Falls Road, 9 miles and turn left at the sign for the Bechler Ranger Station. Drive north 1 mile to the ranger station and trailhead at road's end.

Special note: Campsites cannot be reserved before July 15 but may be available for in-person permits as conditions allow. This hike requires that you have transportation from the Upper Geyser Basin back to your vehicle at the Bechler Ranger Station, a one-way shuttle of 110 miles through Madison, West Yellowstone, and south on U.S. 20 to Ashton.

The hike: You have seen most of Yellowstone—now it is time to explore this remote, often forgotten area. The Bechler River Basin, popularly known as Cascade Corner, receives more precipitation than the rest of Yellowstone, creating a richness of springs, creeks, rivers, waterfalls, and geothermal areas. You will be far from the crowds and close to elk, moose, bears, pikas, gray wolves, beaver, muskrats, river otters, bald eagles, osprey, and waterfowl. In the vast, lush meadows, look for coyotes and sandhill cranes. Along your walk, you will enjoy stunning views of the Grand Tetons to the south.

Day One: Your total distance today will be about 8 miles. From the Bechler Ranger Station, hike north on the Bechler Meadows Trail 3.5 miles to the Bechler River Trail. Continue north on the Bechler River Trail, crossing Boundary Creek on a low-slung suspension bridge. Hike another 4.4 miles to your first night's campsite on the south side of the Bechler River. I recommend 9B5 if it's available when you register. Colonnade Falls, an unusual two-step waterfall, is not far upstream.

Day Two: Try to get an early start—you'll be hiking nearly 13 miles today. Continue northeast on the Bechler River Trail as it threads Bechler Canyon, passing Iris Falls, Ragged Falls, and several unnamed cascades. There's also a geothermal area to explore at Three River Junction. From here, the trail climbs gradually, reaching it's high point at about 8,500 feet. You soon arrive at campsite 9D4 on the Continental Divide about 20.8 miles from the Bechler Ranger Station.

Day Three: You'll cover a little over 7 miles today, nearly all of it on a gentle downhill grade. Head north on the Bechler River Trail. It drops into the Shoshone Creek drainage, then crosses a bridge over the Firehole River. Soon you connect with the Shoshone Lake Trail; turn left and continue north. The Shoshone Lake Trail connects with the Howard Eaton Trail at 24.6 miles. Turn left again and continue north 2.9 miles until you hit a gravel service road. Turn right and walk down the road to a trailhead and parking lot on the west side of the Grand Loop Road adjacent to the Old Faithful area. A path on the other side of the Grand Loop Road leads to the Old Faithful Snow Lodge and cabins.

THE MINIMUM YOU SHOULD KNOW ABOUT YELLOWSTONE'S GEOLOGY

Jim Peaco, National Park Service

Yellowstone is an active volcano!

But where is the cone?

There isn't one; it's a shield volcano. Of the 1,500 active volcanoes worldwide, about 30 are shield volcanoes.

How do we know that it is active?

Park seismographs record as many as 3,000 minor earthquakes each year as the tectonic plate slides over molten rock. The magma column that fuels the hot springs and geysers is about the size of Rhode Island lying between 3 miles and 125 miles below your feet. The earthquakes and geothermal activity attest that Yellowstone is in constant change.

How often does the volcano erupt?

It has erupted at least 100 times in the last 16.5 million years, though most of these are smaller events. Larger, catastrophic eruptions happen on average every 600,000 years. The last big eruption was about 630,000 years ago and left a huge volcanic crater in the center of the park. It is shown on the NPS park map as the caldera.

Will Yellowstone erupt in my lifetime?

Probably not, but if it did, it would change your life regardless of where you live on Earth.

There are more than 10,000 geothermal features in Yellowstone, the most diverse and intact assemblage on the planet. All are driven by a chamber of molten rock from 3 to 5 miles below the Earth's surface. Each feature is grouped into one of four categories: geysers, fumaroles, hot springs, and mudpots. Experience each type to begin to understand the wild, changing nature of Yellowstone.

GEYSERS

There are more than 300 geysers in Yellowstone, the greatest concentration in the world. They range from perpetual spouters, which erupt without stopping, to those that have been observed to erupt only once since 1871. Many are predictable, others are not. Many of the geysers have interconnected plumbing, while a few have no connections to any other geothermal features.

You will observe that some geysers erupt out of cones, while others erupt from pools. Echinus Geyser in the Norris Geyser Basin is a typical pool geyser. Beehive Geyser in the Upper Geyser Basin is a typical cone geyser.

Jim Peaco, National Park Service

Why They Are Here

Geysers are in Yellowstone because several factors come together in this special place. The ingredients needed for making a geyser include: proximity to a chamber of molten rock, a replenishable supply of water that percolates from the heat source to the surface, a very hard volcanic rock known as rhyolite, and enough time for the pressure and chemistry of the hot water to sculpt a unique plumbing system.

How They Work

Surface water percolates into an intricate groundwater network. The magma pool beneath Yellowstone heats the water and through a complex plumbing system forces the water back near the surface. Chambers in the plumbing allow heated water to collect. The water becomes superheated and the pressure it exerts is released through a pipe-like opening to the surface (steam phase). When enough pressure is released, the remaining water in the chamber boils and explodes to the surface (the eruption).

BEST GEYSERS

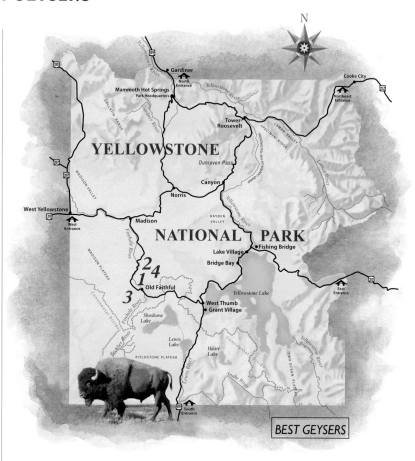

BEST GEYSERS

Yellowstone is a marvel. It has the largest assortment of geysers in the world. Some erupt continuously; others haven't erupted for decades. Look for the unexpected while visiting the geyser basins. With more than 300 geysers, each with a different cycle, the probability of one going off near you at any given moment is good. You may even chance upon a rare event, like the eruption of 200-foot Giantess Geyser in the Upper Geyser Basin.

Geysers are grouped in nine basins near the south, west, and northwest edge of the caldera, which makes up a large part of central Yellowstone. Some go almost unnoticed because they are remote, have irregular eruptions, or are small. Others are world-renowned: Steamboat, the tallest on Earth at 300 feet; Fishing Cone, picturesque on the shore of Yellowstone Lake; and Old Faithful, the most iconic. Here are the must-see geysers that you might experience during a two-day visit.

I. Upper Geyser Basin

Old Faithful

Mention Yellowstone National Park to anyone and the image of Old Faithful Geyser will most likely come to mind. Old Faithful stands alone as a classic geyser. Its predictability, duration of eruption, height of display, beautiful symmetry, and isolation from other features combine to provoke universal awe. Predicted eruption times are posted in the Old Faithful Visitor Education Center.

Riverside

This may be the most beautiful and unique setting of all of Yellowstone's geysers. The cone rises out of the bank of the Firehole River.

Jim Peaco, National Park Service

You watch an eruption from the opposite bank. Rather than spouting vertically, it shoots over the river at a 20-degree angle. Riverside is more consistent than Old Faithful. Free of plumbing attached to any other geysers, Riverside receives a consistent recharge of water. It erupts every 6 to 8 hours, at 75 feet for 20 minutes. Check the Old Faithful Visitor Education Center for the next time it is predicted to play.

Grotto

This geyser is a fascinating feature because of its cavernous cone. The geyser issued forth in the center of a group of trees. The water covered the trees in siliceous deposits that hardened, giving rise to the unique cone. Grotto is worth seeing, even if it is not erupting. It can erupt for up to 36 hours and discharge several times the amount of water of Old Faithful.

J. Schmidt, National Park Service

2. Lower Geyser Basin

Clepsydra

If you entered the park from West Yellowstone or Mammoth and have not yet seen a geyser, consider stopping at the Lower Geyser Basin for Clepsydra. Named after an ancient Greek water

Jim Peaco, National Park Service

clock device, Clepsydra's eruption is almost constant. Known for being in a "wild phase," it jets water and steam to 40 feet. Clepsydra introduces you to the violent nature of geysers.

3. Black Sand Basin

Cliff Geyser

Like Clepsydra, this geyser plays almost nonstop. Whereas you observe Clepsydra from a distance, you can experience the sights, sounds, and rumblings of Cliff Geyser up close from an observation platform. When the wind cooperates, you can feel the steam and spray of this violent feature. Careful! Geyser water deposits silica that permanently coats eyewear and camera lenses.

4. Firehole Lake Drive

Great Fountain Geyser
This is the only geyser on this list that erupts from a crater rather than a cone. It is entertaining to watch the crater steadily fill with water before eruption. As its name implies, Great Fountain is large, erupting to 200 feet. Sunset is a sensational time

Jim Peaco, National Park Service

to catch the waning sunlight though the water and steam. Eruptions are regular enough to be predicted. Times are often displayed near the observation area and at the Old Faithful Visitor Education Center.

GEYSER GAZERS

Some visitors consider themselves "geyser gazers." They dedicate countless hours during their vacations to sit by geysers, recording their activities. They may watch a geyser for several days before it erupts. Then they share their observations with scientists to augment decades of research data, helping identify trends in Yellowstone's ever-changing geothermal areas.

Jo Suderman, National Park Service

Jim Peaco, National Park Service

BEST FUMAROLES

Stan Canter, National Park Service

You know that you are on a volcano when you see a fumarole. The name is from Latin, referring to smoke. Fumaroles are present on active volcanoes during quiet periods between eruptions.

A fumarole is a volcanic vent from which steam and gasses issue. More specifically, a fumarole is the visible evidence of an underground hot spring that boils off all its water before the water reaches the surface. The steam is created when the pressure on this superheated water drops. Then the steam explodes from the surface through cracks in the surface rocks.

A lot of steam escaping from a vent means that the groundwater is near the surface. Gasses typically mixed with steam include carbon dioxide, sulfur dioxide, and the rotten-egg-smelling hydrogen sulfide.

Yellowstone has more than 4,000 unnamed fumaroles; a few others have been given names. The two easiest to view are in the northeast corner of West Thumb Geyser Basin, and the Black Growler Steam Vent in Norris Geyser Basin. You can approach the fumaroles on boardwalks at West Thumb. Black Growler can be viewed from the Porcelain Basin overlook just outside the Norris Geyser Basin museum. Other fumaroles are scattered around the geyser basins.

BEST HOT SPRINGS

Why is the surface of the spring moving? Hundreds of feet below you, groundwater contacts rocks heated by Yellowstone's magma chamber. Water temperature rises above boiling, but does not turn to steam because of the weight of overlying cooler, denser water. The heavier, cooler water sinks and pushes the superheated water toward the surface, producing convection currents that stir the pool's bubbling and roiling water. Hot springs have wide openings, allowing the slow release of water pressure, while geysers have a constricted opening, forcing a fire hose-like release.

The iconic must-see hot springs are Black Pool in West Thumb, Grand Prismatic in Midway Geyser Basin, Morning Glory Pool in

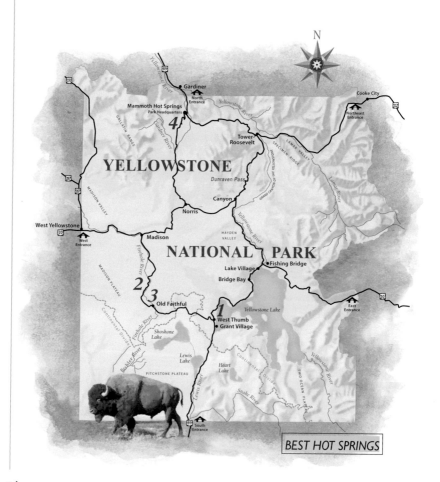

BEST HOT SPRINGS

Upper Geyser Basin, and Mammoth
Hot Springs at Mammoth.

1. Black Pool (West Thumb Geyser Basin)

You will see that the name of this
170°F hot spring does not describe its
cerulean blue color. Most hot springs
appear predominantly blue because
the wavelengths of other colors in the
sunlight spectrum are absorbed by
the clear water. The water scatters
the blue wavelengths, reflecting them
back to our eyes.

2. Grand Prismatic (Midway Geyser Basin)

If you were to view the multicolored

Jim Peaco, National Park Service

Grand Prismatic from above, you would see that it is a distinctive deep
blue. Most of its iconic photos have been taken from aircraft. From
the boardwalk, you will
pass along the edge
of Grand Prismatic,
the park's largest hot
spring. Feel its steam
and marvel at the
colorful thermophile
microorganisms living
in its shallow waters.

Jim Peaco, National Park Service

Jim Peaco, National Park Service

3. Morning Glory Pool (Upper Geyser Basin)

Once a crown jewel renowned for its deep blue hue, the Morning Glory Pool now is more green and yellow. Decades of coins and other debris tossed into the pool have restricted convection currents, cooling the surface water and allowing bacteria to grow. It remains an iconic Yellowstone feature, and a worthy reward for walking the 1.3 miles from Old Faithful Inn.

4. Mammoth Hot Springs (Mammoth)

The northwest corner of the Upper Grand Loop Road passes by a rare natural phenomenon. Here at Mammoth Hot Springs you can witness geologic change happening before your eyes. Rocks are forming. Use your camera; select a spot to photograph where the water flows over a terrace. Return on your next trip to Yellowstone and examine the same location. It will not look the same.

Cracks in ancient limestone allow hot, carbon dioxide–laden water to effuse from the springs. This mild carbonic acid further dissolves the limestone and deposits it on the surface as travertine rock.

Jim Peaco, National Park Service

BEST MUDPOTS

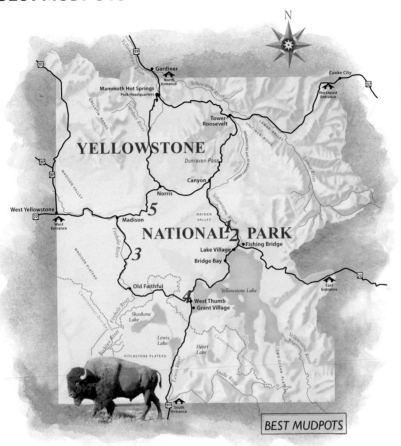

BEST MUDPOTS

Mudpots are hot springs where the water dissolves the surrounding volcanic rock, releasing acids that in turn break down more rock. Mudpots are located in all of the major geothermal areas except Mammoth Hot Springs. The most prominent and easy to access mudpots are in the West Thumb Geyser Basin, Mud Volcano area, Artists Paint Pots area, and the Lower Geyser Basin. Short walks take you to Dragon's Mouth and Mud Volcano, as well as Fountain Paint Pots, and West Thumb Paint Pots. A longer stretch of your legs takes you to the Artists Paint Pots.

1. Dragon's Mouth

From the Mud Volcano parking lot, the pounding sound of Dragon's Mouth hastens you up the boardwalk to see what could possibly be making such a noise. The mudpot's cave-like opening thuds with furious wave action, and steam issues from beneath. The feature has a fitting name.

Jim Peaco, National Park Service

2. Mud Volcano

The sights and sounds of this bubbling spring are hypnotic. Avoid letting any of the mud land on you. The spring's temperature is more than 180°F and the mud is very acidic.

3. Fountain Paint Pots

Located close to the parking area in the Lower Geyser Basin, the Fountain Paint Pots are the most colorful on this list. The thickness of the mud is somewhat seasonal. Regardless of the season, the pinks and grays of this relatively quiet mudpot is an elegant curiosity.

Jim Peaco, National Park Service

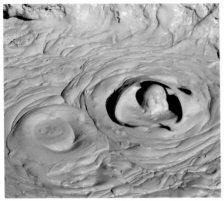

4. West Thumb Paint Pots

The West Thumb Paint Pots are forever effervescent. This feature covers a wide area of the West Thumb Geyser Basin, so you can see it from different angles. The temperature of the mud is almost boiling, yet you'll see vegetation growing right to the edge of the spring.

J. Schmidt, National Park Service

5. Artists Paint Pots

These lovely features are in the Artists Paint Pots in the Gibbon Geyser Basin, 0.5 mile from the parking lot trailhead south of Norris. The paint pots are forever launching colorful mud several feet skyward. Listen to the mud splatter back into the pool.

Mary Meagher, National Park Service

BEST NAMES OF NATURAL FEATURES

Most of the 10,000 geothermal features and small waterfalls are unnamed. Many backcountry streams and lakes have no official name. Here is a list of the most whimsical, lyrical, or descriptive park feature names that you may encounter during your visit.

Mammoth Hot Springs
- Cleopatra Terrace
- White Elephant Back Terrace

Mud Volcano Area
- Black Dragon's Cauldron
- Dragon's Mouth
- Mud Volcano

Upper Geyser Basin
- Beehive Geyser
- Biscuit Basin
- Morning Glory Pool

Lamar Valley

- The Thunderer

Lower Geyser Basin

- Celestine Pool
- Clepsydra Geyser

Midway Geyser Basin

- Grand Prismatic Spring

Mammoth – Norris Road

- Roaring Mountain

Norris Geyser Basin

- Puff 'n Stuff Geyser
- Porkchop Geyser
- Whale's Mouth
- Whirligig Geyser
- Green Dragon Spring
- Hurricane Vent

West Thumb Geyser Basin

- Fishing Cone
- Blue Funnel Spring

Find a geyser, hot spring, mudpot, or fumarole without a name. Give it one.

BEST WATERFALLS

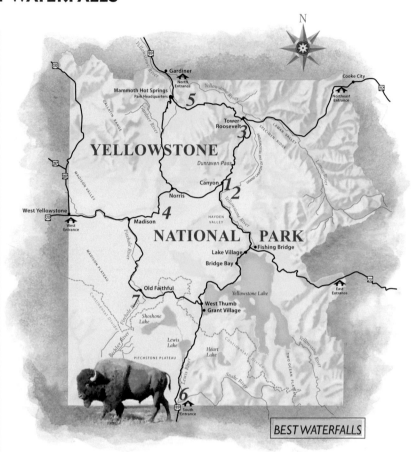

Many of Yellowstone's best-loved iconic waterfalls are a short walk from your car. The must-experience waterfalls are the Upper Falls of the Yellowstone, the Lower Falls of the Yellowstone, and Tower Fall. If you love the sights and sounds of falling water, you should also seek out Gibbon Falls, Undine Falls, Moose Falls, and Kepler Cascades, all readily accessible from park roads. Longer backcountry trails lead to many spectacular waterfalls in the Bechler River region, in the southwest corner the park, accessible by gravel road from Ashton, Idaho.

I. Upper Falls of the Yellowstone River

Feel the rumble and the spray as you stand near the brink of the 109-foot falls. Look upriver at the relative calm before the water reaches the rim. Take your camera; you may capture a rainbow. The two best places to experience the Upper Falls are at the Brink of the Upper Falls and Upper Falls View. The Brink of the Upper Falls turnoff is about 2 miles south of Canyon Village on the Grand Loop Road. The Upper Falls View is off South Rim Drive, 2.5 miles south of Canyon Village.

Jim Peaco, National Park Service

2. Lower Falls of the Yellowstone River

At 308 feet, the Lower Falls is the largest waterfall in the Rocky Mountains, and at peak flow its volume would fill an average house (20,000 cubic feet) every three seconds. In 1872, painter Thomas Moran sketched the falls from the north rim, at a place known today as Moran Point, and his subsequent iconic painting helped persuade Congress to protect the region as a national park. A more popular viewpoint, Artist Point, is reached by following South Rim Drive to its end. The drive is 2.5 miles south of Canyon Village.

Jim Peaco, National Park Service

3. Tower Fall

Visitors marvel at their first sighting of this 132-foot cataract, named for the spire-like rocks between which the creek rushes forth. Once called Tower Falls, the name was changed to singular to denote its unobstructed drop. Trappers and prospectors called it Little Falls, to distinguish it from the Great Falls of the Yellowstone (the combined Upper and Lower Falls). This photo is from the upper viewing area. A 0.25-mile descent along a trail behind this viewing area provides a memorable view of the fall from below. You will find Tower Fall 1 mile south of Tower-Roosevelt Junction.

4. Gibbon Falls

This popular feature is 2 miles east of Madison Junction on the Grand Loop Road. The 84-foot waterfall on the Gibbon River can be seen from a viewpoint next to a large parking area. Ferdinand Hayden named it in honor of Colonel John Gibbon, who brought a small detachment of soldiers to the park in 1872, and was an army commander during the Nez Perce War. He never visited the falls or the geyser basin that were given his name.

5. Undine Falls

An ancient Northern European myth tells of undines (UN-deens), female water spirits, who were created without souls. Marrying a mortal and bearing him a child would lead to their soul's creation. Listen to the falling water and imagine why the falls were named after the mythical beings. You will find Undine Falls 4 miles east of Mammoth on the road between Mammoth and Tower-Roosevelt. A large parking area on the north side provides access to an overlook for you to admire the 60-foot cataract on Lava Creek.

Jim Peaco, National Park Service

6. Moose Falls

From the South Entrance, many visitors bound for more iconic destinations drive past this first major feature. Moose Falls, just 1.5 miles north of the South Entrance, is a mere 0.1-mile walk from the road. The pool at the foot of the 30-foot waterfall along Crawfish Creek is a popular spot for a dunk in the (cold) water.

Diane Renkin, National Park Service

7. Kepler Cascades

Cascades are some of the most furious features, as water is forced through a small canyon to jet over rocks. The 125-foot Kepler Cascades is no exception. Superintendent Philetus Norris named these cascades in honor of "the intrepid twelve-year-old son of Governor Hoyt, of Wyoming, who shared all the hardships, privations, and dangers of the explorations of his father." Kepler Cascades is on the Firehole River, 1 mile east of the Upper Geyser Basin along the Lower Grand Loop Road.

BEST BOATING

Ed Austin and Herb Jones, National Park Service

Yellowstone has two popular boating lakes: Yellowstone Lake and Lewis Lake. You can rent a boat to use on Yellowstone Lake or bring your own. You must bring your own boat to cruise Lewis Lake.

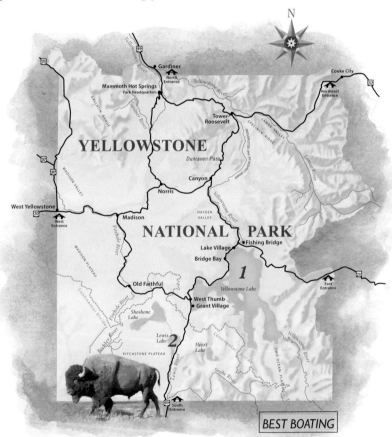

I. Yellowstone Lake

Take a one-hour scenic cruise aboard the *Lake Queen II* to Stevenson Island. The cruise is offered several times daily during the busy summer season. Views of the Lake Hotel before sunset are exceptional. The *Lake Queen II* leaves from Bridge Bay Marina, 3 miles south of Lake Village.

Jim Peaco, National Park Service

Jim Peaco, National Park Service

Would you rather be your own captain? Bridge Bay Marina offers rowboat and motorboat rentals for cruising the shoreline. Watch for waterfowl and look for deer coming to the lakeshore for a drink.

2. Lewis Lake

Bring your own kayak or canoe and explore the shallow waters along the lake's edge. For added interest, you can paddle up the Lewis River from Lewis Lake toward Shoshone Lake. The current can make progress upstream difficult. Well-prepared adventurers with a backcountry permit can spend a night or more at one of the canoe campgrounds on Shoshone Lake.

You'll need to acquire a boat permit if you intend to launch your boat in the park. Caution is needed as lake waters in the park are extremely cold and prone to large waves from sudden storms.

William Dunmire, National Park Service

BEST PLACES TO FISH

Jim Peaco, National Park Service

Yellowstone is an angler's wonderland. Fish of several species abound in the lakes, rivers, and creeks. Some fish populations descend from ancestors occupying the same waters tens of thousands of years ago. Landing one of these wild successors is part of the allure of fishing these storied waters.

Stream Fishing

There are more than 2,600 miles of streams in Yellowstone. Stretched end-to-end they would reach from Los Angeles to New York. Almost all have populations of trout. Cutthroat trout is the only native species; the other trout were introduced into park waters. The best known waterways and the fish that inhabit them are:

Gallatin River: brown trout and rainbow trout

Madison River: brown trout and rainbow trout

Firehole River: brook trout, brown trout, and rainbow trout

Gibbon River: Arctic grayling, brook trout, brown trout, cutthroat trout, and rainbow trout

Lower Yellowstone River: brown trout, cutthroat trout, rainbow trout, and whitefish

Gardner River: brown trout, cutthroat trout, rainbow trout, and whitefish

Lamar River: cutthroat trout and rainbow trout

Slough Creek: cutthroat trout and rainbow trout

Soda Butte Creek: cutthroat trout and rainbow trout

Lewis River: brown trout, brook trout, cutthroat trout, and rainbow trout

Lake Fishing

Yellowstone has about 150 lakes and ponds; nearly half harbor fish. The larger fishable lakes and the populations within include:

Yellowstone Lake: cutthroat trout and lake trout

Heart Lake: cutthroat trout, lake trout, and whitefish

Shoshone Lake: brook trout, brown trout, and lake trout

Lewis Lake: brown trout and lake trout

Trout Lake: cutthroat trout and rainbow trout

You will receive the latest park fishing regulations when you acquire your park fishing permit. It can be obtained at all entrance stations and park concessionaires inside and outside the park.

Bryan Harry, National Park Service

Jim Peaco, National Park Service

BEST FISH

Yellowstone has over 200 waterways and 45 lakes that harbor fish. Some of these waters are home to three iconic native fish: westslope cutthroat trout, Yellowstone cutthroat trout, and Arctic grayling. Other waters host nonnative species include brook trout, brown trout, rainbow trout, and lake trout.

Here are the iconic native fish:

Westslope Cutthroat Trout
Oncorhynchus clarkii lewisi
This species is native to waters west of the Continental Divide.

Jim Ruzycki, National Park Service

National Park Service

Yellowstone Cutthroat Trout
Oncorhynchus clarkii bouvieri
Native to the Yellowstone River drainage.

Arctic Grayling
Thymallus arcticus montanus
Thrives in small, cold, clear lakes and tributaries of the Madison River and the Yellowstone River.

National Park Service

National Park Service

Nonnative species include:

Brook Trout
Salvelinus fontinalis
Native of the northeastern United States and the Appalachian Mountains to Georgia.

Brown Trout
Salmo trutta
Brought from Germany and Scotland, native to Europe and western Asia.

National Park Service

National Park Service

Rainbow Trout
Oncorhynchus mykiss
Native to western North America, but not Yellowstone waters.

Lake Trout
Salvelinus namaycush
Native to Alaska and Canada, now in the cold depths of Yellowstone Lake, Shoshone Lake, and Heart Lake. To help protect native fish, park regulations require that you kill any lake trout you catch in Yellowstone Lake.

National Park Service

BEST MAMMALS

Yellowstone is big enough that its mountains, valleys, rivers, lakes, weather, and seasons mold the lives of its animals. Sixty-seven species of mammals live out their lives in this protected wilderness.

It is a mistake to consider Yellowstone National Park a big drive-thru zoo. It is the heart of a large, intact ecosystem. With the exception of the black-footed ferret, all of the major animal species that were present at the time of Columbus are here today.

The park is famous for celebrated iconic animals, such as gray wolves and grizzly bears. Other mammals are common though less renowned, and a few are notable, such as mountain lions and wolverines, but rarely seen.

Jim Peaco, National Park Service

Every animal in Yellowstone National Park is wild and possibly dangerous. Do not approach any animal. Observe it at a distance that does not change its behavior. This is for your safety and to keep from upsetting the animal. It is illegal to willfully remain near or approach wildlife within any distance that disturbs or displaces the animal.

A CHECKLIST OF YELLOWSTONE'S MAMMALS

___ American Pika	___ Bison
___ Chipmunk	___ Black Bear
___ Yellow-bellied Marmot	___ Grizzly Bear
___ Uinta Ground Squirrel	___ Pronghorn
___ Golden-mantled Ground Squirrel	___ Bighorn Sheep
	___ Mountain Goat
___ Red Squirrel	___ Elk
___ Beaver	___ Mule Deer
___ Coyote	___ White-tailed Deer
___ Gray Wolf	___ Moose

Chipmunk

Least *(Tamias minimus)*
Uinta *(Tamias umbrinus)*
Yellow-pine *(Tamias amoenus)*

Chipmunks are affable squirrels. Few sights are more charming than a chipmunk sitting on a rock with forepaws folded against its chest.

Stan Canter, National Park Service

The genus *Tamias* is Greek for "storer." They do not build fat like ground squirrels, so chipmunks hoard food in underground caches for hibernation. Their periods of dormancy can last from many days to several weeks. They awaken often during winter and feed on their larder. Chipmunks experience little weight loss by the time hibernation ends in April.

The three species in Yellowstone National Park are almost impossible to distinguish by sight. Most field guides tell you to distinguish the chipmunks by counting the number of lines on their backs, but I have found that they move too fast to get an accurate count. I recommend that you identify chipmunks by habitat. Uinta chipmunks live in Yellowstone's abundant lodgepole pine forests. Least chipmunks are plentiful in higher-elevation coniferous forests and alpine tundra. Yellow-pine chipmunks are abundant in the brushy areas of the lower elevations, as well as in rocky places and open forests.

The diet of all three species is similar, consisting of berries, nuts, fruits, flowers, conifer seeds, leaves, grasses, pollen, mushrooms, insects, and bird eggs.

Chipmunks play an important roll in dispersing seeds and expanding plant habitat. They spend much of their day scattering seeds and hiding them in every possible place. Seeds that they fail to retrieve often sprout in new places.

Not by their choosing, chipmunks play an important role as prey for many mammals and birds. If they avoid predators, they can live up to 6 years in the park.

Best Places to See Chipmunks

Look for yellow-pine chipmunks in the Mammoth Campground and Tower-Roosevelt area. You will find Uinta chipmunks throughout the park in coniferous forests. Look for them around Grant Village, Canyon, and Fishing Bridge. Find least chipmunks at Mount Washburn, Dunraven Pass, and Sylvan Pass.

Golden-mantled Ground Squirrel

Callospermophilus lateralis

"They look like 'Chip and Dale!'" Yes, but they are not chipmunks. The Disney animators who drew the beloved cartoon characters must have thought that golden-mantled ground squirrels were chipmunks. Visitors often misidentify ground squirrels as chipmunks. Golden-mantled ground squirrels do not have stripes on their heads, whereas chipmunks do.

These squirrels are accustomed to sharing their habitat with humans, and are common denizens in campgrounds, picnic areas, around lodges, and at scenic turnouts. Golden-mantled ground squirrels that live at high elevations enter their dens fat on seeds, insects, and bird eggs in late August. September is the time for those living in lower elevations to enter their 8-month hibernation. Their scientific name, *Callospermophilus*, is from the Greek *kallos* "beauty," *spermatos* for "seed," and *phileo* for "love."

Best Places to See Golden-mantled Ground Squirrels
You will see these endearing squirrels throughout the park. Look for them where people congregate, around lodges, cabins, and campgrounds.

Roger Wilson, National Park Service

Uinta Ground Squirrel
Urocitellus armatus

Teenagers are often accused of sleeping too much, but it doesn't match the amount of sleep the Uinta ground squirrel gets. These diminutive Rip Van Winkles sleep eight months out of the year.

The Uinta ground squirrel is active throughout spring and summer, feeding on seeds, green vegetation, insects, and sometimes meat, in order to build fat. Uintas live in colonies. Young are born in May and have only two months to grow to adult size. It is so important for young squirrels to grow and build up fat for hibernation that they may not notice you approaching; they are too busy eating.

Like all ground squirrels, they favor cool weather and are intolerant of heat and dryness. By mid-August, most are in their burrows beginning their lengthy hibernation.

Best Places to See Uinta Ground Squirrels
Large colonies flourish in the Mammoth Hot Springs area, around Lake Hotel, and in Canyon Village.

Red Squirrel
Tamiasciurus hudsonicus

The red squirrel is the only daytime tree squirrel in Yellowstone. These tree acrobats will delight you with their endearing antics as they chase each other up and down tree trunks and spring

National Park Service

from tree limb to tree limb. You may detect these squirrels by sight or sound. Their noisy chattering is a territorial cry. With a home range of less than two football fields, and population densities of two squirrels to three acres, their territories easily overlap. They do not like to share their cached food and will fight to protect it. Red squirrels do not hibernate and can live 10 years if they can stay away from owls, martens, foxes, and bobcats.

Best Places to See Red Squirrels

Red squirrels feed on pine and spruce cones, so look and listen for them throughout Yellowstone's forests, particularly around Yellowstone Lake and Lewis Lake. You will also see them in campgrounds at Norris, Madison, Indian Creek, Tower, and Bridge Bay.

American Pika

Ochotona princeps

Like an alpine farmer, American pikas scurry to bring haystacks out of a midsummer thunderstorm. The pika stashes the alpine flowers and grasses it has cut to keep them dry. As every farmer knows, hay molds when wet. When the sun returns, the pika spreads the hay on rocks to dry. Often called rock rabbits, these grapefruit-size mammals sound a short warning squeak when you approach their rocky alpine meadow home. Pikas store hay deep within the rockslide, saving it for food during winter. The pika does not hibernate but stays active in the dark among the rocks under several feet of snow.

Pikas can withstand only a few consecutive hours at temperatures above 70°F. Changes in global temperature have forced pikas to migrate to higher ranges, cutting off access to neighboring populations which in turn reduces their numbers. Like canaries in a coal mine, pikas provide a warning call for the future of many plant and animal species in Yellowstone.

Best Places to See Pikas

You may find pikas near Sylvan Pass, Mount Washburn, Dunraven Pass, and Sheepeater Cliff.

Yellow-bellied Marmot

Marmota flaviventris

About the size of a soccer ball with a tail, yellow-bellied marmots are also known as rockchucks or whistle pigs. They are a member of the

squirrel family and can weigh up to 11 pounds.

Living on rocky alpine slopes, in meadows with rocks nearby, and along cliff faces throughout the park, these grizzled-looking colonial rodents are distinguished by their mock boxing matches, nuzzling of one another, sunbathing, and standing on their hind legs chirping out whistles. They fatten themselves during the summer on grasses and flowers and burn off the fat in hibernation, which accounts for about 60 percent of their lives!

Best Places to See Yellow-bellied Marmots
You might see yellow-bellied marmots at Storm Point, Craig Pass, Firehole Falls, Mount Washburn, Canyon, Sylvan Pass, and along the Madison River Canyon. Remember, they live among the rocks.

Beaver
Castor canadensis

National Park Service

Imagine building a dam across a flowing stream at night. That is what beaver are able to do. The ponds they make allow willows to grow along the shore. Willows are a favored food for beaver. Eventually their ponds fill with silt and become meadows, serving as home to elk, deer, bobcats, and foxes. In the 1800s, demand for luxuriant, waterproof beaver pelts for clothing and hats drove trappers into the Yellowstone area nearly 40 years before the first government expeditions. Almost trapped to extinction, beaver also lost habitat when wolves were exterminated in the park and expanding elk herds over-browsed the willows. Today, there are nearly 500 beaver in Yellowstone; their numbers have rebounded in most areas.

Best Places to See Beaver
Beaver are active in the morning and evening. Find a stream or pond with a beaver dam, gnawed trees, and other signs of beaver activity.

Then wait patiently. The best place to watch for beaver is in Willow Park along the west side of the Mammoth-to-Norris Road just south of Indian Creek Campground. Also, a 5-mile round-trip loop hike leads to beaver ponds from a trailhead north of the Liberty Cap at Lower Mammoth Terraces (see page 46).

Bighorn Sheep
Ovis canadensis

Jim Peaco, National Park Service

The Native Americans who lived year-round in Yellowstone relied on bighorn sheep as their key food source. The Sheepeater band of Shoshoni, the Túkudeka, were moved from the park to a reservation well before the sheep population was depleted. Today, there are about 275 bighorn sheep in Yellowstone National Park. Bighorn sheep like to hang out together, sometimes in groups up to 100. Besides their dramatically curved horns, bighorn sheep rams are known for butting their heads together to determine who is dominant. During mating season, they square off, rise up on their hind legs, tuck their chins, and lunge at each other at 20 miles per hour. The resulting crack of sound can be heard over a mile away in the thin mountain air.

Best Places to See Bighorn Sheep

A group lives in Gardner River Canyon between Mammoth Campground and the North Entrance, and is often seen high above on the rocky crags or crossing the road for water. Another small group stays near Dunraven Pass on Mount Washburn. You may also see them near the East Entrance, on the roadside cliffs just west of Soda Butte above the Northeast Entrance Road, along the Gallatin River Canyon in the northwest section of the park, and at Tower.

Pronghorn
Antilocapra americana

Pronghorn look similar to the true antelopes of Africa, which is why many people call them antelope. Their behavior and needs also are similar. Both animals live in the grasslands, and both are speedy. But the American pronghorn is unique, unlike any other animal on the planet.

Pronghorn are superbly adapted to living in open prairies, where they use their speed to avoid predators. To their benefit, pronghorn can race away at up to 60 miles per hour and maintain half that rate for 6 or 7 miles. Even a week-old pronghorn can outrun a dog. They are the world's

Jim Peaco, National Park Service

greatest marathon land animals. Wolves, mountain lions, coyotes, bobcats, and even raptors rely on pronghorn for parts of their diets.

Best Places to See Pronghorns

Between 200 and 300 pronghorn live in Yellowstone at least part of the year, mostly in the northern end of the park. The best places to see pronghorn are along the one-way gravel Old Gardiner Road from Mammoth to Gardiner, in the hills south of the North Entrance, in open areas along the road from Mammoth to Tower-Roosevelt, and in the Lamar Valley.

Mountain Goat

Oreamnos americanus

Visitors sometimes confuse mountain goats and bighorn sheep. Mountain goats have relatively straight, black horns, while bighorn sheep horns are gray or brown and are deeply

Diane Renkin, National Park Service

curled. Sheep are mostly gray to tan, while goats are white. Where you find them helps you distinguish them, too. Bighorn sheep live on rocky slopes with ample grass, while goats prefer higher, cliff-ridden mountain peaks and ridges.

Mountain goats spend most of their time grazing on grasses, herbs, ferns, mosses, and lichens. When not feeding, they rest on rocky cliffs protected from predators. A sure-footed climber at high elevations, their cloven hooves can spread apart, while their inner pads provide traction to help them navigate steep, rocky slopes.

The common name is misleading; this is not a true goat, but a member of the bovine family. Predation is uncommon. The young are sometimes taken by golden eagles, but only mountain lions are surefooted enough to kill adults. Even that is improbable as mountain goats have a powerful sense of smell and can see movement up to a mile away. Mountain goats are not native to Yellowstone. They moved in after being introduced in the 1940s into the Absaroka-Beartooth Mountains on the park's northern boundary. Today, an estimated 200 to 300 mountain goats live in the park and adjacent areas, where their average lifespan in the wild is 15 years.

ANTLERS OR HORNS?

Horns are bony outgrowths sheathed in keratin, the same material as your fingernails. Horns are found on the heads of bison, bighorn sheep, and pronghorn. Horns are never shed, but remain with the animal for life. Pronghorn, singular creature that they are, do shed the outer sheath, which promptly grows back. Male elk, moose, and deer have antlers. These bone-like substances grow during the warm seasons and are shed after the animals mate in autumn.

Best Places to See Mountain Goats

Look for mountain goats in alpine areas in the northeast and northwest corners of the park.

White-tailed Deer

Odocoileus virginianus

Can you imagine spending almost half of your day eating? White-tailed deer pass more than 40 percent of their day browsing on grasses, brushy plants, twigs, and leaves. You will recognize white-tailed deer by their long white tails, which they wave as a warning signal when wary or frightened. When they need to, they can escape at 30 miles per hour, leap as high as 10 feet, and can cross the Grand Loop Road in a single vault. White-tailed deer are common in Yellowstone and can live 16 years if they avoid wolves and mountain lions.

National Park Service

Best Places to See White-tailed Deer

Look for white-tailed deer where you see their larger cousin, the elk. Although less common in Yellowstone, you may see them along the Madison River near Madison Junction, the Lamar River and its tributaries, and in the Lava Creek-Gardner River Valley.

Mule Deer

Odocoileus hemionus

Disney animators selected the mule deer to be the beloved Bambi in the popular motion picture. It is the most common deer you will see in Yellowstone. Larger and darker colored than white-tailed deer, they

National Park Service.

are recognized by their large "mule" ears, their short tail with black markings, and their bounding gait on all four legs as they escape trouble.

Like their cousin the white-tailed deer, mule deer are browsers. Yet where their habitats overlap, their diets vary enough that they are not in direct competition for food.

Mule deer live up to 11 years in the park if, as adults, they avoid mountain lions and wolves, and, as fawns, they are fortunate enough to also avoid coyotes, eagles, bears, and bobcats.

Best Places to See Mule Deer

Mule deer are plentiful in the park. Look for them around Canyon, Mammoth, Lake, Madison, the geyser basins, and along the road between Mammoth and Norris.

Rocky Mountain Elk

Cervus elaphus nelsoni

If it looks like a deer, but it is much larger than either a mule deer or a white-tailed deer, then it is an elk. They can be almost as large as a moose! The best time to see large numbers of elk is in the

Jim Peaco, National Park Service

autumn when they migrate to lower elevations in the north end of the park. It is at this time that the bulls compete with one another as they collect their harems. The sound of bulls bugling on a frosty October morning to attract cows provokes a feeling of wild grandeur.

During summer, elk travel in small groups and favor the forests. There are about 15,000 elk from six or seven herds residing in Yellowstone during the summer. That number drops to less than 5,000 that over-winter in the park. They can live up to 14 years when protected in a wild place like Yellowstone. Because bulls can live to an advanced age, they can develop huge antler racks.

Best Places to See Rocky Mountain Elk

Elk are almost always present in the Mammoth Hot Springs area. You will also find elk in the Lamar and Hayden Valleys, on Mount Washburn, near Norris Junction, along the West Entrance Road, and around the Upper Geyser Basin.

Moose

Alces alces

How would you like to carry 60 pounds on your head for seven months? Mature moose bulls can live up to 20 years and carry antlers that can span 5 feet and weigh 60 pounds. Females do not have antlers, but like the bulls have a "bell," or dewlap, which is the flap of skin and long hair that hangs from the throat; no one knows the purpose of the dewlap.

The gawky-looking moose is the largest member of the deer family. They can swim as fast as two men paddling a canoe and run nearly as fast as the speed limit on park roads. Be careful if you come across a moose;

THE MULTIFACETED MOOSE...

Jeff Foott, National Park Service

- can swim 6 miles per hour for up to 2 hours,
- can dive up to 20 feet underwater,
- can run up to 36 miles per hour for short distances,
- can run as far as 15 miles without stopping,
- can stay underwater for more than a minute,
- has hollow hair that helps it float,
- has front teeth only on the bottom jaw,
- eats about 40 to 60 pounds of food a day.

they can be irritable and have been known to attack people, horses, cars, snowmobiles, and road maintenance machines.

Best Places to See Moose
There are fewer than 100 moose living in the park. Look for them in marshy areas and meadows during spring and summer. You will find moose in forested areas as winter progresses. You might also see a moose while hiking to Riddle Lake (see page 54), Shoshone Lake (see page 55), or Cascade Lake (see page 52).

Bison

Bison bison

The American bison is the most emblematic animal of the wild American West. (Look for the bison profile on the National Park Service patch.) They evolved in Euro-Asia during the Pleistocene era and migrated to North America about 12,000 years ago. By the time Europeans arrived on the continent, as many as 60 million bison roamed the grasslands and forests as far east as Pennsylvania; south to Florida's panhandle, Louisiana, Texas, and northern Mexico; north on the plains in Saskatchewan and Alberta; and west to northern California. Now, about 15,000 wild bison roam North America; almost 3,500 live in Yellowstone. They are the largest land animals on the continent.

HOW FAST CAN THEY RUN?

Jeff Foott, National Park Service

How would you match up in a race? The following are maximum speeds of the animals found in Yellowstone National Park. Some can be sustained over long distances while others represent short sprinting speeds.

Red squirrel: 12 mph
White-tailed deer: 30 mph
Bison: 40 mph
Black bear: 33 mph
Mule deer: 35 mph
Mountain lion: 35 mph
Moose: 36 mph
Snowshoe rabbit: 38 mph
Grizzly bear: 40 mph
Coyote: 43 mph
Gray wolf: 45 mph
Elk: 45 mph
Pronghorn: 60 mph
Maximum driving speed in the park: 45 mph
Fastest Olympic sprinter: 27 mph

If you were an Olympic sprinter, you could outrun a red squirrel.

Look for bison in herds, small groups, and as single animals. They often seem to be resting, and therefore harmless, but be aware. Weighing

up to half as much as your car, these seemingly docile animals are unpredictable and quick, able to run up to 40 miles per hour. Each year, more people are injured by bison than by bears. One summer I saw a bison bull attack a tour bus, mashing the front bumper into the wheel, disabling the bus.

Linda Duvanich

The best times to see bison are during their courtship rut in August, calving season in May, and throughout the winter. After a snowstorm their coats are covered in snow, making them difficult to spot.

Best Places to See Bison

Free roaming, bison are found throughout the park, especially in the Lamar and Hayden Valleys, along the road from Mammoth to Tower-Roosevelt, and from West Yellowstone to Old Faithful.

Coyote
Canis latrans

Yip, yip, yip! It usually starts with one melodious yip in the night. In less than a minute, several more coyotes will join the chorus. Coyotes are numerous and live in every imaginable part of the West, from wilderness to

Jim Peaco, National Park Service

urban areas. Considered undesirable by many, they are adaptable and able to thrive despite extermination efforts in some areas. No longer hunted in Yellowstone, today they are plentiful throughout the park.

Visitors often mistake a coyote for its bigger cousin, the gray wolf; a coyote's ears and nose are more pointed. You may encounter a coyote trotting down a road in front of your car. Look for one in grasslands hunting rodents. If you don't see a coyote, listen for its yelping at night.

Best places to see coyotes

Coyotes blend well with grasses and sagebrush, but you may spot one in the Lamar and Hayden Valleys, Gardners Hole, the North Entrance, roadside meadows along the Madison River, and Blacktail Plateau Drive.

Gray Wolf
Canis lupus

Lords of the canine world, gray wolves again roam Yellowstone. Predator control efforts in the early 20th century

Jim Peaco, National Park Service

reduced overall numbers until the packs were destroyed. Recent enlightened policy led the National Park Service to reintroduce wolves in 1995 and 1996, and return Yellowstone to a wild ecosystem. Alone, wolves eat small mammals and birds; in packs, they prey on deer, moose, and elk, herbivores that have over-browsed grassland

CANINE COUSINS

Jim Peaco, National Park Service

A flash of something bolting across the road ahead, and your brain registers a familiar object: a domestic dog. Immediately thereafter, your brain reminds you that there shouldn't be border collies on the loose in Yellowstone. It must be another canine, but what? You saw one of three canine cousins: a fox, a coyote, or a wolf. Here's how you might be able to tell the difference between these Yellowstone inhabitants the next time a dog dashes in front of you:

A fox has red fur and long, thin, dark legs for its relatively small size of about 10 pounds. A coyote is often tan or gray, and looks more like a medium-size domestic dog, topping out at about 35 pounds. Also, compared to wolves, foxes and coyotes have pointier ears and noses. A gray wolf is black, gray, or even white, and is two to three times the size of a coyote, weighing as much as 120 pounds.

Coyotes and foxes are seen throughout the park, while you would more likely see wolves in Lamar Valley, Hayden Valley, near Mount Washburn, and in Gardners Hole.

and aspen forest communities. The wolves have prospered, aspen groves are returning, and grasslands are becoming more diverse.

PREDATOR CONTROL

Jim Peaco, National Park Service

A program began in 1915 to eliminate coyotes, mountain lions, grizzly bears, wolverines, lynx, bobcats, and wolves from Yellowstone. These predators were considered threats to nearby ranch operations, and to the animals that visitors most wanted to see: deer, moose, and elk. By 1935, most of the predator populations were shattered, and the control programs had ended. Deer and elk numbers began to rise and soon became too large, over-browsing some forests and grasslands.

Predator populations gradually recovered, and the ecosystem began to repair. The reintroduction of gray wolves in 1995 brought a more complete wildness back to Yellowstone.

Although you may not see a wolf, you can still listen for one. The howl of the gray wolf can travel 10 miles. As afternoon light fades in the Lamar Valley, listen for the long, sorrowful howl of the gray wolf. Its cry brings chills—and perhaps more howls from nearby wolves—and reminds you that you are visiting a true American wilderness.

Best Places to See a Wolf

About 100 gray wolves roam select territories in Yellowstone. Look for them in the Lamar and Hayden Valleys, and Swan Lake Flats. Do you want current information about Yellowstone's wolves? Visit the Yellowstone Association visitor center in Gardiner. The Association maintains the best up-to-date information on each of the packs, and some of the individual wolves, including photographs!

Black Bear
Ursus americanus

Black bears are common in Yellowstone National Park. Their coloration can be black, blue-black, cinnamon, brown, blond, and almost white.

Bryan Harry, National Park Service

They evolved in forest environments and are excellent tree climbers. Black bears are also solitary, wandering territories of 15 to 80 square miles. Considered opportunistic eaters, their diet includes grasses, roots, forbs, nuts, berries, insects, fish, and small mammals. Black bears are extremely adaptable and can develop a preference for human foods and garbage. Bears who become attracted to human food can become aggressive.

When autumn snows arrive, black bears seek a cave, burrow, or tree cavity to make their dens. They have also been known to find shelter in crawl spaces under buildings. Bears pass the winter in a state of dormancy, awakening when disturbed, and may leave their dens for brief periods.

Harlan Kredit, National Park Service

During the park's long winters, bears live on body fat they stored by gorging all summer and fall. Huckleberries are critical to their health, supplying great amounts of sugar in the fall that turns to fat.

Females give birth to two or three blind, helpless cubs in midwinter and nurse them in the den until spring. Mother and cubs will stay together for about two years. The life expectancy of a black bear in Yellowstone National Park is up to 20 years.

Best Places to See Black Bears

All of Yellowstone is bear country, but the best places to look for black bears are along the edges of wooded areas in the Mammoth Hot Springs area and near Tower-Roosevelt.

Jim Peaco, National Park Service

Grizzly Bear
Ursus arctos

Grizzly bears are peerless. With no natural enemies, they are the monarchs of the wild. They can weigh 400 to 700 pounds, and can outsprint a horse. Yet you may be surprised that fully 85 percent of this feared predator's diet consists of fruits, grasses, roots, bulbs, and whitebark pine nuts. The remainder of their diet is ground-dwelling rodents, insects, fish, elk calves, and carrion.

YELLOWSTONE'S GRIZZLIES

Jim Peaco, National Park Service

Grizzly bears can run up to 40 miles per hour. It is a myth that they are unable to run downhill. In truth, they can run as fast downhill as they can uphill. They are also very good swimmers. Their eyesight is on par with humans (and far better than ours at night), and they have an excellent sense of smell.

Nature has painted the estimated 600 Yellowstone grizzly bears with myriad colors. They can be blond, brown, nearly black, and almost white. Meriwether Lewis called grizzlies the "white bear."

Grizzlies are wild animals and can be unpredictable and dangerous if you surprise them, if they think you threaten their cubs, or if you get close to their food. Consider yourself fortunate if you see a grizzly. Make sure that you observe it at a distance that will not change its behavior. Remember, you are a guest in bear country.

Best Places to See a Grizzly Bear

All of Yellowstone is grizzly country, but the best places to look for one are the Hayden Valley, east of Fishing Bridge to the East Entrance, on the slopes of Mount Washburn around Dunraven Pass, and in the Lamar Valley.

Jim Peaco, National Park Service

BEST PLACES TO SEE WILDLIFE FROM THE ROAD

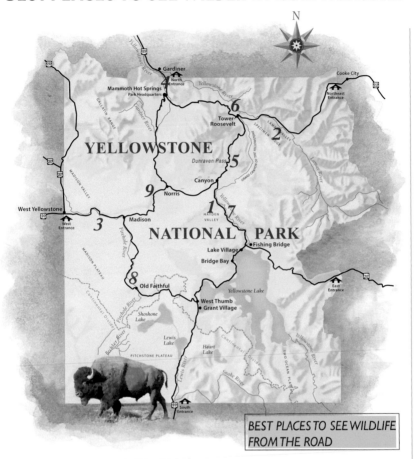

BEST PLACES TO SEE WILDLIFE FROM THE ROAD

Where can you see wildlife in Yellowstone? Any place and any time—the entire park is wildlife habitat. A sure sign of wildlife is a cluster of people huddled around spotting scopes and tripod-mounted cameras on the side of the road. (Always park off the road and use official pullouts when stopping to view wildlife.) Many animals are most active in the hours around dawn and dusk, so plan your day accordingly. Bison, elk, and pronghorn often graze in the open, while predators and smaller animals tend to favor the edges where forest and meadows meet. Moose prefer the dense cover of willow stands. Also watch streambanks and the shorelines of lakes and ponds.

I have often seen a bear crossing the roadway right after a vehicle passes. Be sure to check your rearview mirror. Ask passengers in your

Jim Peaco, National Park Service

vehicle to watch for wildlife on both sides of the road. You can see many things happening around you when you are paying attention! Sometimes the best strategy is to park in a pullout with a wide field of view over one of Yellowstone's broad valleys. Scan near and far, using binoculars if you have them, and stay alert for movement. Patience and being mindful of the sights and sounds around you often pay off with memorable wildlife sightings. A bison herd with newborn calves is a treat to see, and the scene may also attract wolves or bears. No wolves on the distant ridge today? Perhaps not, but don't miss the family of coyote pups playing outside their den just below the road. Here are some of the best places where you might find specific animals.

1. **Hayden Valley:** bison, grizzly bears, gray wolves, elk, coyotes
2. **Lamar Valley:** bison, grizzly bears, gray wolves, elk, coyotes
3. **West Entrance Road from Seven-Mile Bridge to Madison Junction:** elk, bison, trumpeter swans
4. **Gardner River Canyon:** bighorn sheep
5. **Dunraven Pass:** bighorn sheep
6. **Tower-Roosevelt Junction:** black bears
7. **Yellowstone River from Fishing Bridge to Chittenden Bridge:** white pelicans
8. **Upper Geyser Basin to Nez Perce Picnic Area:** bison
9. **Elk Park (south of Norris):** elk

BEST BIRDS OF YELLOWSTONE

Observers began collecting data in 1872 on bird species observed in Yellowstone. To date, 330 have been identified. The National Park Service now estimates that there are 148 species nesting here. Casual travelers will likely see few of these. But given the large number of feathered animals living in the park, you can't avoid happening upon some. The more difficult or rare birds to find include the peregrine falcon, common loon, and nocturnal owls. Birds that are common but often overlooked are the mountain bluebird, western meadowlark, and common merganser. Robins, crows, and ravens are abundant and seen throughout the park, any time of year. Several other species are representative of the Mountain West, and have a special connection to Yellowstone. You may encounter these by staying alert.

A CHECKLIST OF BIRDS YOU MAY SEE OR HEAR

- ____ Clark's Nutcracker
- ____ Mountain Chickadee
- ____ Black-capped Chickadee
- ____ Bald Eagle
- ____ Osprey
- ____ Trumpeter Swan
- ____ American Dipper
- ____ Ruffed Grouse
- ____ Gray Jay
- ____ Canada Goose
- ____ Sandhill Crane
- ____ American White Pelican
- ____ Black-billed Magpie
- ____ Steller's Jay

Canada Goose
Branta canadensis

Ask someone to visualize a goose, and they will no doubt picture a Canada goose—the most common goose in America.

Canada geese adapt to any habitat where grasses, grains, and berries are available. This

J. Schmidt, National Park Service

explains why the species is so widespread. Also, a successful protection program in the early 1900s reversed population declines due to overhunting. The birds were protected by law and even reintroduced in some areas.

Historically, the geese summered in Yellowstone and migrated south each autumn in large, noisy flocks honking their way along centuries-old flight paths. Their characteristic "V-shape" is well known. Many birds continue that cycle. Others have learned that the long migration is unnecessary, as they have become acclimated to the available food in the park during the cold seasons. You shouldn't be surprised to find Canada geese in winter drifting about in iceless pools and waterways.

Best Places to See Canada Geese
You will encounter Canada geese throughout the park wherever there is standing or moving water. You are almost assured of seeing them along the shores of Yellowstone and Lewis Lakes, and the upper Yellowstone, Firehole, and Madison Rivers.

Trumpeter Swan
Cygnus buccinator

Linda Duvanich

Visitors are often in awe when they first see a trumpeter swan. This largest of native North American waterfowl is a marvel. Swans can weigh up to 32 pounds and stand 4 feet tall, with a wingspan of up to 8 feet! Named for their trumpet-like call, the birds can live up to 30 years in the wild. Few birds would have lived that long between 1600 and 1900, however. Trumpeter swans were hunted for their large flight feathers, which were considered to make the best quality quill pens. Fortunately for the swans, technology made quill pens obsolete.

Best Places to See Trumpeter Swans
You can expect to find pairs of trumpeter swans along the Madison River, upper Yellowstone River, and lower Firehole River.

American White Pelican
Pelecanus erythrorhynchos

… I measured this pouch and found it's [sic]contents 5 gallons of water
MERIWETHER LEWIS, AUGUST 8, 1804, WRITING ABOUT THE PELICAN

Some historians wonder how the meticulous Lewis and his Corps of Discovery assistants could be so incorrect. Present calculations indicate that an American white pelican holds about three gallons in its pouch. The journals of Meriwether Lewis and William Clark are replete with references of Corp of Discovery members killing white pelicans as they traveled through the northern plains and mountainous areas of Montana, presumably for food.

Stan Canter, National Park Service

Lewis and company would have been measuring the volume of a pelican's pouch in late season, just before the bird left its breeding ground for either the shallow coastal bays of the Gulf of Mexico or southern California. Whether in the north during the summer or in the south for winter, white pelicans live on crayfish, tadpoles, salamanders, and fish.

The wild Molly Islands in the Southeast Arm of Yellowstone Lake are set aside as a protected breeding area for American white pelicans. No boats are allowed within 0.5 mile of the islands. Here, the pelicans make a nest in a shallow depression with a low rim made of gravel, soil, and nearby vegetation. Here, too, they fledge their young, safe from human interference.

Best Places to See White Pelicans

Second only to trumpeter swans in size, white pelicans outperform them as graceful fliers, either singly or in formations. They're also at home in the water. You may see pelicans along the upper Yellowstone River, at Yellowstone Lake, Fishing Bridge, Pelican Creek, Lewis Lake, and along the Madison River.

Harry Engels, National Park Service

Sandhill Crane

Grus canadensis

It's springtime, and you are riding through the Hayden Valley when a curious spectacle catches your attention. Near the Yellowstone River, two birds standing chest-high are flapping their wings, bowing, leaping straight up, and throwing sticks in the air. The sight is mesmerizing.

You are witnessing the mating dance of a pair of sandhill cranes. Listen; the mating might be accompanied by their distinctive rattling *kar-r-r-r- o-o-o* call, which can be heard miles away. This is known as "unison calling," as they face each other and throw their heads back to sing. The dance is done not only during mating season. Single birds and pairs will dance any time of year.

Sandhill cranes nest in Yellowstone each summer. As autumn arrives, they migrate to Florida, Texas, Arizona, Mexico, or California. During their 20-year lifespans, they feed on plants, grains, mice, snakes, insects, and worms in wet grasslands and marshes, like those in the Hayden Valley.

Best Places to See Sandhill Cranes

You may see sandhill cranes during the summer in Fountain Flats, Hayden Valley, and Lamar Valley.

Ruffed Grouse
Bonasa umbellus

You are walking through a forest that has dense undergrowth. Without warning, you hear a thunderous explosion in the leaves a few feet in front of you. Startled, you stop short. Is it a bear? No, you have just experienced a ruffed grouse escaping your presence.

The grouse was aware of you. But this chicken-size bird is so well camouflaged on the forest floor that it flees danger only at the last moment. As you watch what some people call a fools hen escape, you notice it flies little better than a chicken. And if it lands in the bough of a spruce tree, you will notice it is not very good at standing in trees, either.

Once you hear the grouse's distinctive low-pitched drumming, it's fun to look for grouse to watch how a male attracts a female. He performs a wing-beating ritual while standing on a hollow log. He begins by slowly beating his wings front to back as if he intends to fly. In a few moments, the log echoes the drumming sound that increases in speed.

Best Places to See Ruffed Grouse

Look for ruffed grouse in the open forested areas of Mount Washburn, Blacktail Deer Plateau Drive, and Gardners Hole.

Black-capped Chickadee
Poecile atricapillus

Like a sentry, a black-capped chickadee sounds the predator alarm for others in the flock. The more *dee* notes in a *chickadee-dee-dee* call, the higher the threat level. Researchers have found that pygmy owls provoke the most *dees*, as high as 17.

National Park Service

Chickadees spend much of the day picking small insects such as caterpillars off trees. They do not migrate, but flock and travel in large foraging groups.

When food is abundant, they hide seeds and other food, and can remember thousands of hiding places. Every autumn, some of their brain neurons containing old information die and are replaced with new neurons that help them adapt to changes in their social flocks and their environment.

As you walk through forest groves, listen for the high-pitch, two-tone call of the chickadee. Do they see you as a threat? Count the number of *dees* in their call.

Best Places to See Black-capped Chickadees
You will see chickadees throughout the park in lodgepole pine and spruce-fir groves.

Jim Peaco, National Park Service

Mountain Chickadee
Poecile gambeli

As you walk through spruce-fir forests, listen for the high-pitch, two-tone whistle of the chickadee calling its name *(chickadee-dee-dee)*. They also have a call that sounds like they are saying "cheese-bur-ger."

Locate a mountain chickadee and you will see it is not alone. They travel in pairs or small groups during the summer, acrobatically clinging to small limbs or hanging upside down from pine cones as they feed on insects and seeds. Wintertime finds them flocking with black-capped chickadees, nuthatches, and brown creepers, following each other one by one from tree to tree searching for seeds. When you find a mountain chickadee, look to see if it has traveling companions.

Best Places to See Mountain Chickadees
These birds live throughout the spruce-fir forests of Yellowstone. Look for them around Yellowstone Lake, Grant Village, and Lewis Lake.

American Dipper
Cinclus mexicanus

Look for bird droppings on the boulders in fast-moving creeks. These droppings tell you that dippers are living in the area. Listen for the *zeet* call. Also known as a water ouzel, American dippers are

National Park Service

gray and about the size of a young robin with a short tail. They get their name from their bobbing behavior when standing on rocks. They build their nests out of mosses near fast-moving water, often behind waterfalls. Their strong yellow legs allow them to walk underwater to catch aquatic insects and larvae such as mayflies, caddisflies, and mosquitoes. Dippers are fun to watch as they walk into swiftly moving water and disappear. You can only guess where they will emerge.

Best Places to See American Dippers
Dippers are year-round residents living near fast-moving water in the warm months, and moving to lakes and larger rivers with open water in the winter. Look for them at Wraith Falls, below Virginia Cascades and Kepler Cascades, in the Gardner River, and near Lewis Falls and Moose Falls.

Steller's Jay
Cyanocitta stelleri

Like its eastern cousin the blue jay, the Steller's jay is noisy. The bird's intonations are often mistaken for the screams of eagles and hawks. The jay's range of vocalizations is remarkably broad, including scratchy sounds and mimics of other birds, chirping squirrels, meowing cats, wailing dogs, cooing chickens, and even mechanical objects. Steller's jays are sociable, traveling in groups. Watch them playing with or chasing each other within the forest canopy. Year-round residents, they stash pine seeds for winter food.

Jim Peaco, National Park Service

Best Places to See Steller's Jays

Steller's jays live throughout the park and are often found where there is a closed forest canopy.

Gray Jay
Perisoreus canadensis

These medium-size forest denizens glide silently through the conifers, and before you know

Richard Lake, National Park Service

it, a group has encircled your picnic table or campsite. Also known as "camp robbers," these amiable birds can become a nuisance as they attempt to take your food. They are found throughout Yellowstone year-round. Nesting begins in March, with snow on the ground and temperatures as low as -20°F. Females protect the eggs with their thick plumage and a well-insulated nest. They are omnivores that hoard food by using their sticky saliva to glue food bits to tree branches above the height of the eventual snow line.

Best Places to See Gray Jays

Yellowstone has 52 picnic areas and 12 frontcountry campgrounds. These are the best areas to look for gray jays. But don't be tempted to feed them!

Clark's Nutcracker
Nucifraga columbiana

A Clark's nutcracker hides tens of thousands of seeds each year.

Unlike your neighborhood squirrel, the bird has a good memory and can remember where to retrieve the seeds, even nine months later. However,

it occasionally fails to find some of its cached seeds. These seeds sometimes germinate, thereby advancing the forest. Nutcrackers cache all varieties of pine seeds, including whitebark pine. The seeds of the whitebark are rich in calories and consumed in great quantities by bears as they fatten for hibernation. Unfortunately,

Jim Peaco, National Park Service

beetle infestations have affected whitebark pine, significantly reducing the number of trees. Nutcrackers are instrumental in maintaining forest balance by unwittingly planting seeds.

Stashing food allows this year-round resident to begin nesting in late winter. Both the male and female incubate the eggs. Each takes its turn while the other departs to feed at one of their seed caches.

Best Places to See Clark's Nutcrackers

Clark's nutcrackers are altitudinal migrants. As soon as the young fledge in late spring, the family relocates to subalpine habitats up to 11,000 feet. They migrate back to the valleys in the autumn. Some places that you might see them during the height of the visitor season are Craig Pass, Sylvan Lake, Bunsen Peak, and Mount Washburn.

Black-billed Magpie
Pica hudsonia

I had an acquaintance who took a fledgling magpie from its nest and raised it as a pet. It made a mess of his apartment, but it showed me that they are sociable and entertaining companions.

Jim Peaco, National Park Service

Many visitors from outside the Northwest are startled the first time this colorful long-tailed bird zips before their windshield. The bird might be racing to capture a small animal or insect. Their diets are broad, and also include fruits, seeds, and even carrion. These flashy relatives of jays and crows keep up a constant stream of raucous calls when they gather over a meal.

Black-billed magpies associate with people. Meriwether Lewis declared that magpies raided their tents for food. Keep your food properly stored, or you might be inviting an unwelcome friend for a meal.

Best Places to See Black-billed Magpies

Magpies are omnivorous ground feeders who live in open woodlands and meadows. Look for them in the Lamar Valley, Gardners Hole, Mammoth, and the Lake Area.

Osprey

Pandion haliaetus

One of the most spectacular sights you will witness in Yellowstone is an osprey plunging into a lake and carrying a fish in its talons back to its nest. Once called fish hawks, they are unique because their diet is almost exclusively live fish, which they catch by a vertical dive from great heights.

Jim Peaco, National Park Service

Listen for the whistling or chirping calls of an osprey when near lake shorelines. The bird might be calling from its large nest atop a snag or while in flight. Look for its distinctive flight profile: a V-shaped wing silhouette. Watch one for a while, and see if it locates and plunges for a meal.

Osprey are large predators, but strangely, the otherwise humble Canada goose will sometimes take over an osprey nest in the early spring. The goose will successfully fight to keep the osprey away while it uses the nest.

Best Places to See Osprey

Osprey are common in the park. You have a good chance of seeing them at Yellowstone Lake, Lewis Lake, Shoshone Lake, the lower Madison River, and along the upper Yellowstone River and in the Grand Canyon of the Yellowstone. Artist Point is a good place to scan the Grand Canyon for osprey.

Linda Duvanich

Bald Eagle
Haliaeetus leucocephalus

"Sea eagle, white head" is the translation of this bird's scientific name. At the time of naming, "bald" meant white, not hairless. The bald eagle was designated as the official emblem of the United States in 1787 because of "its long life, great strength, and majestic looks," and also because it was believed to exist only on this continent. A robust debate preceded the designation, as political leaders, including Benjamin Franklin, disapproved, stating that the bald eagle was of "bad moral character," proposing, instead, the wild turkey as the national bird.

Best Places to See Bald Eagles

Bald eagles are mostly fish-eating birds. Look for them along lakes and rivers in the summer. During winter and early spring, bald eagles feed on winter-kill bison, elk, and deer. This may have contributed to Franklin's distaste for the bald eagle.

NOTABLE INSECTS

When you think of Yellowstone's iconic animals, you probably do not consider insects. Although you might view some of them as nuisances, they play vital roles in the park's ecology. Unimaginable numbers of insects pollinate most of Yellowstone's wildflowers, trees, and shrubs, and are an integral part of forest succession through infestation. They are also food for countless birds, reptiles, fish, and mammals. Many of the insects migrate during a part of their life cycles beyond the park, underscoring to us that Yellowstone is a wilderness larger than its political boundary.

Grizzly bears spend much of their time in the rocky, alpine meadows of the Absaroka Mountains during late summer. The bears go there to escape the heat, to locate rocks with salt-rich minerals, and to find highly nutritional army cutworm moths and ladybug beetles, key elements to the bears' survival.

Army cutworm moths surface from the prairie soils of Kansas, Nebraska, and Wyoming in late June. Soon after, they fly to the alpine reaches of the Rocky Mountains to avoid summer heat. At night, they feed on flowers; during the day, they hide under small rocks. Grizzly bears know that the moths, though only half a calorie each, are more nutritious than large prey and easier to catch. Like dogs in search of buried bones, the bears scoop with their paws as many as 40,000 moths per day. Look for overturned rocks and logs; a bear may have had a feast!

Ladybug beetles also arise from the prairies and migrate to the mountains. In September, some rocks are so covered in beetles that grizzly bears lick ladybugs up by the mouthful. Beetles that the bears do not eat crawl under the rocks and go into hibernation until June. Why do the ladybugs come to the peaks? In contrast to the windswept prairies, the alpine zone's deep snows provide vital insulation all winter long, allowing the beetles to survive. The ladybugs migrate back to the prairies by June.

Mosquitoes abound in Yellowstone during the warm months. You can find swarms of them in cool, damp areas as well as on warm, sunny hillsides. What are they good for? Mosquitoes are important because they pollinate plants. Only female mosquitoes bite animals. They seek blood protein needed for their eggs to develop. Female mosquitoes are attracted to carbon dioxide. They can sense the carbon dioxide you exhale. Long sleeves, pants, and socks, and a bandana tied around your neck that has been sprayed with a repellent are most effective for keeping mosquitoes from biting. If you do get a mosquito bite, even with all your precautions, just consider it a vacation souvenir.

The native mountain pine beetle can be found infesting lodgepole pine trees and whitebark pine forests. Pine beetle larvae burrow under the bark and eat their way around the tree, cutting off the flow of nutrients. Beetles and their larvae are nutritious to woodpeckers, which feast on them. Infested trees soon die, their needles turning brown or a rusty red. Pine beetles have killed thousands of Yellowstone's trees, making them tinder for fires. The fires cleanse the forest of beetles, the forest regenerates, and the cycle continues. Mature mountain pine beetles emerge from their hosts in midsummer, leaving exit holes that ooze pitch. The pitch accumulates on the surface in crusty mounds. Look for "pitch tubes" on lodgepole pine trees. These trees are infected and will die within months.

Mayflies, stoneflies, salmonflies, and caddisflies are groups of aquatic insects that are critical to Yellowstone's ecology. They feed on plant matter that falls into rivers and streams, breaking down and redistributing the nutrients for other organisms. A great variety of terrestrial, flying, and aquatic animals prey upon them. And because they are hypersensitive to pollution, scientists monitor their numbers and use the results as a barometer for the ecosystem's health.

National Park Service

INVASION!

Jim Peaco, National Park Service

Ten percent of the 1,700 species of plants in Yellowstone are nonnative; their seeds arrive by wind, with stock feed, or attached to clothing, pets, and vehicles.

Animals can be invasive, too. In the 1940s and 1960s, USDA Forest Service personnel introduced mountain goats to some of the rocky cliffs of the Absaroka Range and Beartooth Mountains in Montana. The goats dispersed within the Greater Yellowstone Ecosystem, finding suitable habitat within Yellowstone National Park.

Park managers know that Yellowstone is subject to climate changes and vulnerable to invading species. Present-day management policy follows the 1916 Organic Act establishing the National Park Service, *to conserve the scenery and the natural and historic objects and the wild life therein and to provide for the enjoyment of the same in such manner and by such means as will leave them unimpaired for the enjoyment of future generations.* This mandate requires park service personnel to discourage the invasion of alien species and, where appropriate, remove them.

Diane Renkin, National Park Service

BEST WILDFLOWERS

RG Johnsson, National Park Service

In 1835, fur trapper Osborne Russell ventured into the Yellowstone area and noted, "I would spend the remainder of my days in a place like this where happiness and contentment seemed to reign in wild romantic splendor."

Since Russell's observation, many changes have come to the greatest wildlife sanctuary in the United States, but the flowers would remain wild. A field of glacier lilies always provokes wonder—how do they break through the snow to bloom? You may chance upon an enchanted floral sight that occurs for just a few days every several years. Take the opportunity to stop and admire.

There are almost 1,150 species of vascular plants native to Yellowstone. The most iconic wildflowers are glacier lilies, fringed gentian, paintbrush, and lupine. Several others that you might encounter along the trails, roadways, and in the geothermal areas are monkeyflower, silky phacelia, fireweed, and monkshood.

Ninety-seven percent of Yellowstone is wilderness. If you venture into these wild areas, you will see the romantic splendor that Russell wrote about, rendered in bloom.

Calypso Orchid
Calypso bulbosa

This orchid is also known as fairy slipper, or lady's slipper. Its names suggest delicate beauty. They live no more than five years, and are becoming rare outside

National Park Service

the park because their preferred habitat—mature old-growth forest—is disappearing and the plants are susceptible to disturbance.

Where You Can Find Calypso Orchids
Look for calypso orchids blooming during May and June in cool, deep-shaded forest areas.

Columbine
Aquilegia spp.

This perennial has plenty of cousins. There are between 60 and 70 species growing in North America. The common name columbine comes from Latin for "dove." Someone imagined the resemblance of five doves clustered together in the inverted flower. One species, *Aquilegia coerulea*, is Colorado's state flower.

Where You Can Find Columbine
You will find several varieties of columbine thriving in meadows and woodlands throughout the park.

Fireweed
Chamerion angustifolium

This fast-growing perennial rejuvenates disturbed areas. Autumn is a good time to witness fireweed seeds floating considerable distances across the landscape. Its rapid colonization brings striking pink color to burned areas, roadsides, and other areas where soils have been disturbed. Fireweed increases soil nutrients essential for plant succession and provides food for deer, elk, and grizzly bears.

JW Stockert, National Park Service

Where You Can Find Fireweed
Look for fireweed blooming along the roads and trails throughout the park from late June through September.

JW Stockert, National Park Service

Fringed Gentian
Gentianopsis thermalis

Fringed gentian's flawless splendor provoked the National Park Service to select it as the official flower of Yellowstone. Even before, it captured the attention of poets for centuries. It has inspired well-known writers such as:

William Cullen Bryant
Thou blossom bright with autumn dew,
An colored with the heaven's own blue,

Emily Dickinson
...and just before the snows there came a purple creature that ravished all the hill.

and

Henry David Thoreau
It came very near not being an inhabitant of our latitude, perhaps our globe, at all.

Where You Can Find Fringed Gentians
Look for fringed gentians growing singly and in groups throughout meadows, along lakeshores, and in the geyser basins. They flower from May through late September.

Glacier Lily
Erythronium grandiflorum
Capable of generating heat through stored carbohydrates, glacier lilies can melt snow, pushing through the last inch or two to bloom. Called snow lilies in some places, their bulbs are tasty to rodents and bears, while deer, elk, and bighorn sheep consume their seedpods. These delicate plants can withstand Yellowstone's winter, but not the weight of even a child's step. The slightest pressure will kill the bulb.

Ed Austin and Herb Jones, National Park Service

Where You Can Find Glacier Lilies

Look for glacier lilies blooming near Sylvan Pass, Dunraven Pass, and in the Lake area from May through June.

Harebell
Campanula rotundifolia

According to European folklore, harebells grew in places that hares lived, and witches used its flower juices to change themselves into hares. Hence its common name.

This delicate-looking flower is quite hardy and found throughout Yellowstone. It is adapted to a variety of habitats and can be found in full sun or shade, dry or moist soils, and in forests, meadows, cliffs, and lake beaches, as well as sprouting in roadside gravel.

Where You Can Find Harebells

Everywhere, from lower elevations to high mountain slopes.

Heartleaf Arnica
Arnica cordifolia

The genus name is Greek and refers to the resemblance of the soft hairy leaves to a lamb's ears. Heartleaf arnica plants are important in the life cycles of many butterfly and moth species, as their larvae feed on the leaves.

Where You Can Find Heartleaf Arnica

Look for this perennial blooming in moist, rich soil from June to August. The best growing conditions allow them to form a loose carpet of cheery bright flowers in shady, moist areas.

JW Stockert, National Park Service

Huckleberry
Vaccinium membranaceum

The official fruit of Idaho, huckleberries are an important food for black bears and grizzly bears. The fruit ripens in the high mountains from August to mid-September. The bears depend on the high sugar content in the berries to help them put on fat for winter hibernation. If pregnant bears do not get enough sugar from the huckleberries, they will give birth to fewer cubs. If you see bears foraging on bushes in late summer, they are likely gorging themselves on huckleberries.

Linda Duvanich

Where You Can Find Huckleberries
Huckleberries thrive in the partial shade and acidic soils of conifer forests, so the species is fairly widespread in Yellowstone. Look for huckleberries on north- and east-facing slopes with sandy or gravelly soil.

Lewis Monkeyflower
Mimulus lewisii

The common name refers to the flowers resembling small monkey-like faces. *Mimulus* denotes an actor in a farce or mime, and *lewisii* honors Meriwether Lewis of the Corps of Discovery. Their favored habitat is along streambanks at higher elevations.

Where You Can Find Monkeyflowers
You will find these bright flowers blooming near geothermal areas, creeks, and riparian meadows around Yellowstone Lake from May to September.

Lupine
Lupinus sericeus

White says "Yes," magenta says "No" to nectar-seeking bumblebees. New flowers have white spots on their upper petals, indicating that the nectar is fresh. As the flowers age, the spots turn magenta, telling the bees the nectar is past prime. Bumblebees feed on the freshest flowers, thereby transferring only the best pollen.

Look for the small droplet of water in the center point of each leaf after a rain or morning dew.

Where You Can Find Lupine

Lupine plants have a wide distribution in Yellowstone. They prefer sunny openings in Lamar Valley, Hayden Valley, and around Mammoth Hot Springs.

Monkshood
Aconitum spp.

The genus name is Greek, meaning "without struggle." There are dozens of species of monkshood in the Northern Hemisphere; all are poisonous. Herbalists have known about the toxic properties of this plant since the 1600s. One of its common names is "wolf's bane" because people once extracted its toxins to kill wolves.

Where You Can Find Monkshood

You will find the best examples of monkshood growing throughout moist meadows. Forest-dwelling monkshood plants tend to be tall and gangly as they reach for the light.

J. Schmidt, National Park Service

PAINTBRUSH Castilleja spp.

Texas folklore tells of Little Gopher, an unhappy child because he was not good at running, shooting, and riding and would never be a brave. He feared that he would amount to little until a shaman tells him that everyone has something to contribute. Someday he would learn what he offers.

Several years later, he has a Dream-Vision during which he is told that he will record the events of his tribe for his people to remember. He is shown what he needs to paint the stories, but he realizes that he is missing the vibrant colors needed to show the sunset. One night, he receives another vision that the paints he needs will be provided on a hilltop the next morning. Arriving at the spot, he finds brushes of all colors sticking up from the ground. He paints the

Ed Austin and Herb Jones, National Park Service

most beautiful sunset and leaves the brushes on the hill. The next day, the People find that the brushes have rooted and turned into the paintbrush plants that we now enjoy.

Paintbrush

Castilleja miniata

The Wyoming state flower is found in many colors, including red, orange, yellow, and white. This showy perennial is named for its colorful, ragged bracts that appear to have been dipped in paint. Hummingbirds seek its nectar, leading some botanists to theorize that paintbrush plants and hummingbirds co-evolved.

Don't look for paintbrush in your local nursery. A slow grower, it does not domesticate well. Paintbrush also tends to parasitize the roots of other plants to obtain nutrients.

Ed Austin and Herb Jones, National Park Service

Where You Can Find Paintbrush

The hills, meadows, and roadsides of Yellowstone are ablaze with paintbrush throughout the warm seasons.

Shooting Star

Dodecatheon spp.

Shooting stars are "buzz pollinators." They release pollen from their stamens only from violent shaking. A visiting bumblebee releases the pollen with its vibrating wings. The bee eats some of the pollen and transfers even more to the next shooting stars that it visits.

Where You Can Find Shooting Stars

You will find shooting stars flowering in early June near geothermal areas, streambeds, and around Yellowstone Lake.

Bryan Harry, National Park Service

Silky Phacelia

Phacelia sericea

Silky phacelia is one of the most photogenic and easily recognized wildflowers in Yellowstone. The common name comes from the silvery, fine, short hairs that cover the stems and leaves.

Where You Can Find Silky Phacelia

Look for silky phacelia in July and August along the road at Dunraven Pass.

BEST TREES

Seven coniferous tree species are native in the park, but there are some hardy deciduous trees as well, such as aspen and cottonwood. Look for these and the most iconic cone-bearing trees in Yellowstone: lodgepole pine, Douglas-fir, subalpine fir, Engelmann spruce, and whitebark pine.

Ever-Changing Forests
As you tour Yellowstone, you will see that, in places, the park is covered with trees. Five tree species that are native to Yellowstone make up two predominate forest environments. These are the lodgepole forests and the spruce-fir forests. Both woodlands undergo change, but at different rates.

Lodgepole Pine Forest
Severe wind events that blow down swaths of trees and frequent recurring wildfires open the lodgepole forest for regeneration. Lodgepole pine trees have an advantage over other species because their seeds are the first to germinate after a fire. This, and the park's poor soils, are reasons why lodgepole trees dominate the forested areas in Yellowstone.

Spruce-Fir Forest
Moist, cool, high-altitude environments and nutrient-rich soil offer Engelmann spruce and subalpine fir trees ideal conditions to flourish. You will find these mixed, dense shaded forests around Yellowstone Lake and Lewis Lake. Less susceptible to fire and wind events, the spruce-fir forests seem to change little over the years.

Quaking Aspen
Populus tremuloides

Quaking aspen is the most widely distributed tree species in North America. Their lightweight seeds are wind-scattered great distances. Seedlings become pioneer trees in moist and disturbed areas. Once established, they can propagate by their roots, forming large dome-shaped groves with the older trees in the center. Look for these genetically identical tree islands in the Lamar Valley. Aspen leaves turn a brilliant yellow and orange each autumn, painting Yellowstone's groves with liquid sunshine.

Jim Peaco, National Park Service

Cottonwood

Populus angustifolia
(narrowleaf cottonwood)
Populus tricocarpa
(black cottonwood)

Jim Peaco, National Park Service

What are those big trees lining Fort Yellowstone? Cottonwoods. These very fast-growing trees were planted decades ago to provide shade, a windbreak, and ornamentation. Cottonwood trees are found in protected valleys, canyon bottoms, along streams, at the edges of ponds, and in moist meadows. They are easy to establish, and were a good selection for transplanting to the fort.

About 70 percent of these trees in Yellowstone are narrowleaf, and 30 percent are black cottonwoods. The populations of both began to collapse with the predator control programs that targeted gray wolves. As wolf numbers diminished, elk populations rose. Over the next seven decades, there were more elk to browse young cottonwood trees, thereby reducing the groves. Cottonwood groves began to rebound after the 1995 reintroduction of wolves into the Greater Yellowstone Ecosystem.

Today, you can enjoy their brightly colored yellow leaves each autumn in the Lamar Valley, as well as at Fort Yellowstone.

Douglas-fir

Pseudotsuga menziesii

The Douglas-fir, often called Doug-fir, is misnamed; it is a pine. But the name persists.

Doug-fir trees are central to wildlife needs in Yellowstone. They grow at lower elevations, particularly

JW Stockert, National Park Service

in the northern part of the park. The seeds within the cones are a feast for squirrels and countless insects. After the cones open, they litter the surrounding area.

A Blackfeet story tells that mice tried to hide in Douglas-fir cones

WHAT GOOD ARE DEAD TREES?

From any direction that you entered the park, you would have noticed areas of standing dead trees. Some were killed by fire, some by beetles, and others by changes in geothermal activity. Sometimes called "snags" (an old Scandinavian word for "stump of a tree"), these dead trees are critical to ecology.

Snags provide homes, nesting areas, and shelter during storms to myriad animals. The tallest snags provide the best animal shelter. These "skyscraper"

Harry Engels, National Park Service

habitats limit predator access to roosting and nesting wildlife. Here is a list of ways that snags help wildlife:

- Eagles, herons, osprey, and hawks perch and nest on the tops of snags
- Woodpeckers and brown thrashers feed on insects in the wood
- Bats roost and birds nest under overhanging loose bark
- Woodpeckers, nuthatches, ducks, owls, and squirrels nest in snag cavities

Nationwide, 85 percent of all bird species use snags for nesting, shelter, or food. Nutrients bound in snags begin to recycle when wind and weather send them crashing to the ground. Snags that fall into creeks, marshes, and lakes help create spawning areas for fish and habitat for aquatic insects that then become food for fish.

RG Johnsson, National Park Service

to avoid detection of the pre-human spirit, Naapi. Look for the shape of mice tails and hind legs protruding from the cones. It is a good way to identify the species.

Engelmann Spruce
Picea engelmannii

The trees that you see at timberline include Engelmann spruce. They survive in the highest and coldest areas of the park, tolerating -50°F. Engelmann

Christine Duchesne, National Park Service

spruce trees living at lower elevations, especially along creek bottoms, can grow to 150 feet tall over the span of 400 years. Do you own a piano? The fine-lined, lightweight, and straight wood grain of Engelmanns is ideal for piano sounding boards. Yellowstone's trees are protected from harvesting, so piano manufacturers get their wood from sources on private and national forest lands.

Lodgepole Pine

Pinus contorta

Not unlike people, lodgepole pine trees are prone to natural life-threatening events at about 80 years of age. The infirmities of old age and constant attack by pathogens leave them vulnerable to disease. The weakened trees become more susceptible to fire.

Lodgepole pines evolved as a fire-dependent species. Most of their cones are covered in a wax that melts above 130 degrees, releasing the seeds. They are the

Bob Stevenson, National Park Service

first cone-bearing tree seeds to germinate following a fire. The process is so effective that the new trees often grow clustered closely together, giving rise to the expression a "doghair" stand of trees.

After 1900, some locals dubbed the forest along the first 7 miles of the West Entrance Road "Christmas Tree Park." Short lodgepole pine

Portland National Incident Management Organization

LODGEPOLE PINE

Pinus contorta *("contorted pine")* is a scientific name that belies the straight and long appearance of these trees. The botanists who first identified the characteristics of lodgepole pine were studying specimens growing on the Pacific Coast. There, the lodgepole growth pattern is affected by salt air and wind, causing them to twist and bend. Shorepine is the common name of the coastal trees. It was several years later that botanists learned that shorepine and lodgepole are geneti-

Harry Engels, National Park Service

cally the same. Nonetheless, the species retains the scientific name that describes it as a contorted tree.

In the Rocky Mountain West, lodgepole pine trees often grow so straight that people use the trunks for construction. You'll see lodgepole pines framing tepee lodges, cabins, and the Old Faithful Inn.

trees were growing there after a recent fire. That forest burned again in 1988. Seeds were released during that fire and the area regenerated. What you see now is similar in appearance to how it looked in the early 20th century.

Most of the trees that burned in the 1988 fires were lodgepole pines; they made up about 80 percent of the trees in the woodlands. Look for "doghair" throughout the park. Fire will return as these trees age, and the cycle of refreshing the forests will continue.

Subalpine Fir

Abies lasiocarpa

A popular Christmas tree, subalpine fir is a forest pioneer on disturbed sites. Along with lodgepole pine, fir saplings help to

Frank Walker, National Park Service

rehabilitate the landscape after a fire by reducing erosion, protecting watersheds, and providing cover for wildlife. Subalpine firs are adapted to Yellowstone's coldest temperatures. Heavy snow loads press lower branches to the ground, sometimes bending even the trunks of young trees, providing tent-like cover for hares, lynx, and bobcats. You can identify subalpine fir trees by their cones, which grow upright like candles.

Jim Peaco, National Park Service

Whitebark Pine
Pinus albicaulis

Whitebark pines grow at high elevation and have a special relationship with Clark's nutcrackers, red squirrels, and bears. The birds and squirrels cache pine seeds throughout the forest, and bears raid these storehouses for the energy-rich food. Where whitebark pine thrive, the seeds are a favored and important food for grizzly bears. Any seeds not eaten may germinate, helping spread stands of whitebark pine.

In recent years, infestations of nonnative blister rust (a fungus) and pine beetles have taken a toll on the park's whitebark pine forests, killing young and old trees alike. This means fewer pine seeds, so bears and other wildlife struggle to find enough nourishment to survive long winters. Researchers are monitoring the park's whitebark pine trees to learn more about their role in the complex web of life.

YELLOWSTONE IN WINTER

Visualize an enchanted scene in which the trees and mountains before you are blanketed in sparkling snow. The morning after a storm passes is often cloudless, calm, and cold, offering a sublime spectacle of nature. Few people experience Yellowstone at these times, but those who do have memories that a camera can only partially capture.

Local residents quip about the winter running from September to July. Indeed, winter-like weather is common year-round here. It can snow every month of the year! Deep winter snow closes all roads to automobiles except the Gardiner-Cooke City road, which is plowed. Those who snowmobile, snowshoe, or cross-country ski can tour other reaches of the park. Accommodations are available at the Snow Lodge in the Upper Geyser Basin, Mammoth Hot Springs, and in gateway communities.

We think of winter weather extremes as being unbearable. Few people ever experience temperatures as cold as Yellowstone's record low of -66°F. On average, the coldest month is January, with a mean low temperature of 9°F. The average snowfall across the park is 72 inches, with January receiving the most snow. Some of the high alpine mountaintops receive several feet of snow, while low-lying valleys get a few inches. These conditions are tolerable for most of Yellowstone's wildlife. The plants and animals that you see are adapted to Yellowstone's wide weather variations.

Lodgepole pine, subalpine fir, and Engelmann spruce trees are able to withstand sustained temperatures of -40°F. The life cycles

The Rendezvous Ski Trails outside West Yellowstone are groomed, as are some trails in developed areas within the park. Sometimes you can ski on trails packed by previous skiers. If exploring backcountry routes, you may have to break your own trail. Bring skis and boots made for backcountry touring or mountaineering. Light touring and racing skis do not have enough surface area to break trail.

Stay on the marked trails. It is easy to get lost in fog or snowstorms. Look for the orange metal trail markers attached to trees. Always ski with companions. Stay clear of geothermal features. The snow in geothermal areas is often icy, and what appears to be bare ground may be thin crust overlying scalding water.

You will see wildlife. Keep your distance. Animals are under stress during the winter. If you cause them to move, it forces them to burn costly calories that they need to survive.

Weather changes happen within minutes at this altitude. A clear mild morning can turn deadly cold with high winds by the afternoon. Carry extra clothing, food, water, matches, flashlight, and a whistle. Tell someone where you are going, by what route, and when you plan to return.

Finally, you will want to record your ski adventure with pictures. Cold camera batteries do not function. Keep your camera warm, tucked within your clothing.

The National Park Service provides downloadable maps of the ski trails at www.nps.gov/yell/planyourvisit/skiyell. The maps include Mammoth, Northeast, Tower, Old Faithful, West Entrance, and Canyon areas. Choose your favorite area, and explore Yellowstone's other season.

of perennial grasses and flowers allow them to take advantage of short growing seasons, outcompeting annual plants that require longer summers. Long-lived perennial plants have stored enough nourishment in their roots and stems to give them a head start, growing even as winter lingers. Some, like the glacier lily, begin to grow under the snow.

Non-hibernating animals are also well adapted to conditions that we find unlivable. Pikas need an alpine climate and thrive on temperatures that we call frigid. And during the summer, they can live only a few hours in temperatures in the upper 70s°F. The jumble of rock that they live in gives them protection from what we would think of as a comfortable temperature.

Deep snow may be a problem for us, but not for ptarmigans. Skies often clear after a cold front dumps snow, and temperatures can to drop to record lows. Ptarmigans react by diving headlong into the fluffy snow and ruffling

Jim Peaco, National Park Service

their feathers to make an air pocket. Their body heat keeps the cavern warm, while a few inches above, it may be many degrees colder.

Gray wolves have an easier time catching prey such as white-tailed deer when the snow is deep enough to slow the deer's escape. As winter snows accumulate, deer have more difficulty escaping the wolves.

Many animals rest in hibernation, while others stay active beneath the snow or on the surface. Animals that you might see in winter are bison, elk, white-tailed deer, mule deer, coyotes, eagles, trumpeter swans, and gray wolves, all of which may be seen along the road between Gardiner and Cooke City. Look for bison between the Seven-Mile Bridge and the Upper Geyser Basin if you travel by snowcoach or snowmobile from West Yellowstone. Winter is the best time to see the iconic primordial images of bison, their long coats encrusted in snow.

BEST SKI TRAILS

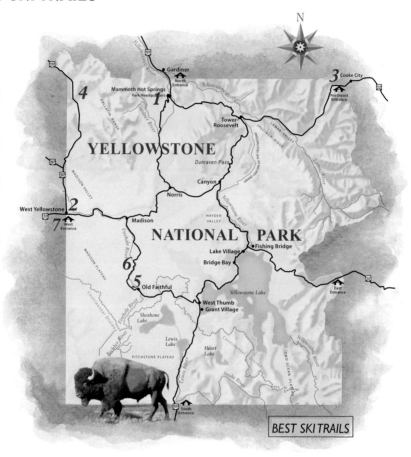

BEST SKI TRAILS

Do you cross-country ski? If so, the Yellowstone region is for you. The National Park Service and the community of West Yellowstone maintain or have marked several ski trails, some of them requiring only novice skills. The following are some of the best easy trails for providing you with the solitude of winter and excellent exploration opportunities. You can get to the trailheads at Mammoth, the West Entrance, Northeast Entrance, and Northwest Yellowstone by automobile all winter. All other trails require access by snowcoach.

Jim Peaco, National Park Service

1. Mammoth

Upper Terrace Loop Trail
Drive to the barricade on the Mammoth-Norris Road. This trail follows Upper Terrace Drive. View the Lower Terraces from the overlook. Ski past Orange Mound Spring, White Elephant Back Terrace, and Angel Terrace.

2. West Entrance

Riverside Trail
This easy trail begins in West Yellowstone at a break in the fence on Boundary Street at the east end of Madison Avenue. The trail follows a power line to an old service road and then follows the road. The "Upriver" and "Downriver" loops combine for 6 miles of trail, with great views of Mount Holmes and the Gallatin Range. Look for bison, elk, deer, and moose. Bald eagles and trumpeter swans frequent the area.

3. Northeast Entrance
The Barronette Ski Trail is an easy, 3.7-mile, one-way trip following Soda Butte Creek at the base of Barronette Peak. The area gets ample snow and is accessible throughout the winter from the Northeast Entrance Road. A 2.5-mile extension of the trail runs between Falls Creek and the community of Silver Gate, where you can purchase supplies and refreshments.

4. Northwest Yellowstone
Few people realize that U.S. Highway 191 from West Yellowstone to Belgrade, Montana, passes through the northwest section of Yellowstone National Park for 31 miles. The highway provides access to several trails for your skiing pleasure.

Daly Creek Trail—Black Butte Trail Loop
The best trail for the novice skier in this corner of the park is this 7-mile loop. This is a popular route for cruising on spring mornings. This loop offers a breathtaking adventure, filled with stunning natural beauty. Access the Daly Creek Trailhead 30 miles north of West Yellowstone off U.S. Highway 191. The first 2 miles of the trail run through rolling meadows. At 2 miles, you reach the Black Butte Trail Cutoff to your right. Follow the cutoff past the Daly Creek backcountry patrol cabin another 2

miles to the Black Butte Trail. Again, turn right and ski the undulating trail through forests to the highway. From the Black Butte Trailhead, ski north 1.2 miles on the east side of the highway to return to the Daly Creek Trailhead.

Jim Peaco, National Park Service

5. Upper Geyser Basin

The trails from the Upper Geyser Basin and Lower Geyser Basin require access by snowmobile or snowcoach. Because of snowcoach schedules, it is best to stay overnight at the Snow Lodge. Serious skiers stay two nights to explore the 40 miles of cross-country trails here.

Black Sand Basin Trail

Imagine skiing among roaring and steaming geysers! This 4-mile one-way trail begins in front of the Old Faithful Visitor and Education Center, climbs Geyser Hill, and then runs down toward Morning Glory Pool. Take the turnoff left to the Daisy Geyser Group and continue on this trail until you come to the Grand Loop Road and Black Sand Basin. You will ski past some of the most iconic geysers and hot springs on Earth.

Biscuit Basin Loop Trail

This is one of the most popular ski trails in Yellowstone because it is an easy loop. The 5-mile route begins across the road from Old Faithful Snow Lodge and continues through the Upper Geyser Basin. Follow the trail to Morning Glory Pool and beyond to Biscuit Basin. This trail passes by many geothermal features, with good possibilities of viewing elk and bison. Complete the loop by following the Mystic Falls Trail a few yards, then turn left onto a trail that leads down to a footbridge across the Little Firehole River. From the bridge, the trail continues through the woods and meadows for about a mile, returning to the main trail through the Upper Geyser Basin near Grotto Geyser. Turn right for the Snow Lodge and a warm refreshment.

Lone Star Geyser

Inquire at the Old Faithful Visitor Education Center for a prediction when the geyser will erupt next on its three-hour cycle. Begin this 9-mile trail across from the Old Faithful Snow Lodge. The trail follows Mallard Lake Trail through the Old Faithful Lodge cabin area and crosses the Firehole River. Follow an old road cut to the Grand Loop Road. Ski southeast until you see orange markers directing you into the woods. After 1 mile, the trail returns to the Grand Loop Road at Kepler Cascades. The trail continues along the east bank of the Firehole River and follows an old service road to Lone Star Geyser.

6. Lower Geyser Basin

Fairy Falls Trail

The trail is an easy 11 miles round-trip, with a total of only 160 feet change in elevation. The route begins at Old Faithful Snow Lodge and travels through the Upper Geyser Basin. Pass Morning Glory Pool and continue north to Biscuit Basin. Follow the trail that parallels the Grand Loop Road until you reach the Fairy Falls Trailhead at the southern end of Fountain Flat Drive; continue on that trail. At about 1.3 miles, the trail divides. Ski to the left, passing through the lodgepole pine forest to Fairy Falls. You will find that the ice-encrusted waterfall is one of the most spectacular winter sights in the park. Retrace your tracks to the Snow Lodge.

7. Outside the Park

The Rendezvous Ski Trail System from West Yellowstone offers more than 20 miles of world-class trails winding through Gallatin National Forest. The trailhead is on Obsidian Avenue on the southwest corner of town in West Yellowstone. Trails are professionally groomed for both skating and classic skiing from November through March. A pass (available at daily, multiday, monthly, and seasonal rates) is required to use the Rendezvous trails. Passes can be purchased at the trailhead, USDA Forest Service ranger district office, West Yellowstone Chamber of Commerce, or at several outdoor sports shops in town.

BEST THINGS TO DO ON A RAINY (OR SNOWY) DAY

Diane Renkin, National Park Service

The average elevation of Yellowstone National Park is 8,000 feet. Weather can be dramatic and raw in this thin air. That innocent cloud to the west can turn a warm sunny day to a cold rainy one in minutes. A bright August morning could end with a snowy afternoon. Accept the drama as a fact of being in Wonderland. Make the most of wild weather with the following activities.

- Photograph the stormy conditions; they make some of the most interesting images.

- Park in a pullout in the Lamar or Hayden Valleys and watch wildlife from your car. Stormy weather sends most humans indoors, but other animals carry on their outdoor lives.

- Bundle up and take a stroll in a steamy geyser basin or at the Mammoth Hot Springs Terraces. (Careful, the boardwalks are slippery when wet.)

- Enjoy live music in the evenings at Old Faithful Inn.

- Spend time at the Old Faithful and Canyon Visitor Education Centers.

David Restivo, National Park Service

Curl up with your favorite book in the lobby at Lake Hotel, Old Faithful Inn, or Mammoth Hotel.

Tour the Albright Visitor Center in Mammoth to learn about the history of the park.

Check out the historic ranger station at Norris (now a museum) to see how early day rangers lived.

Visit the historic trailside museums at Madison Junction and Fishing Bridge for their unique parkitecture and the interpretive stories within.

Watch Old Faithful erupt from a comfortable chair under the big eave on the balcony of the Old Faithful Inn.

Watch people and the weather from the Lake Hotel lobby.

Head for the cafeterias at Lake Lodge, Old Faithful Lodge, or Roosevelt Lodge to watch the weather from their large windows while you enjoy a warm meal or refreshment.

BEST ACTIVITIES FOR CHILDREN

Teaching children about the natural world should be treated as one of the most important events in their lives.
– Thomas Berry

Yellowstone National Park is like no other place on Earth. Its long list of astonishing phenomena makes it exceptional among the world's national parks. The park was set aside for everyone, not just adults. Here is a list of activities you can do with your children to increase their awareness of Yellowstone National Park, and to reveal its wonders and build lasting memories.

Designed Programs

The National Park Service has three programs designed to help children discover the wonders of Yellowstone. Kids can participate in the Junior Ranger Program, "Let's Move *Outside*" initiative, and become a "Young Scientist."

Explore, learn, and protect as a Junior Ranger! Yellowstone National Park's Junior Ranger Program is designed to allow children to explore the park at their own pace. Kids attend a ranger-led program and complete at least five activities in a Junior Ranger booklet. Junior Ranger badges are awarded to a child when a park ranger checks the youngster's finished booklet. Booklets are available at the Madison and Fishing Bridge Trailside Museums, Albright Visitor Center in Mammoth, the Canyon Visitor Education Center, Grant Village Visitor Center, West Yellowstone Visitor Center, and the Old Faithful Visitor Education Center. Look for Junior Ranger Station Activities at Madison, and the Junior Ranger Discovery Program at Grant Village. You can also participate online at the National Park Service's WebRangers site: www.nps.gov/webrangers/.

The National Park Service also offers the "Let's Move *Outside*" program, which is intended to help kids develop an active lifestyle. Children who hike along park trails and boardwalks, with a ranger or family, or participate in the "Yellowstone Wildlife Olympics" will earn a "Let's Move *Outside*" sticker or temporary tattoo to proudly display.

Investigate Yellowstone as a scientist. Purchase a self-guiding booklet and check out a "Young Scientist Toolkit" from either the Canyon

Visitor Education Center (ages 5 and up), or the Old Faithful Visitor Education Center (ages 10 and up). Complete the investigation activities and be awarded a Young Scientist patch.

Pick Up a Free Activity Book

Yellowstone's primary concessionaire gives away a free activity book, just for kids. Find them at any Xanterra dining room.

Ride a Bicycle

There are several designated bicycle paths in Yellowstone National Park. Two of the best for children are the Old Faithful to Biscuit Basin Trail in the Upper Geyser Basin, and the Fountain Freight Road in the Midway Geyser Basin. The 2.3-mile (one-way) Old Faithful to Biscuit Basin Trail has both paved and gravel sections and takes you past many of the most sensational features in the Upper Basin. Didn't come prepared with a bicycle? No worries. You can rent bicycles from the gift shop in the Snow Lodge. The 2.75-mile one-way Fountain Freight Road in the Midway Basin is an easy ride along an abandoned freight road. A side trip to Fairy Falls is possible, but you must walk the 1.6 miles to the falls from the trailhead. Bring a lock for your bike.

Fish at Trout Lake

It is an easy 0.6-mile round-trip walk from the Northeast Entrance Road to 12-acre Trout Lake, which is famous for cutthroat trout and rainbow trout. A park fishing permit is required; check in at a visitor center or ranger station before angling. For those in the family who do not fish, the scenery is splendid, and a 0.8-mile trail loops around the lakeshore. Watch for river otter and other wildlife.

Attend an Evening Program

Learn about the fascinating diversity of Yellowstone National Park with the help of an experienced park ranger. Topics include bears, birds, history, climate change, and of course geysers! Review the park newspaper and select a campground amphitheater presentation at Fishing Bridge, Bridge Bay, Madison, West Yellowstone, Grant Village, Norris, Old Faithful, or Mammoth.

Attend a Ranger-led Program

The National Park Service offers a variety of ranger-led programs especially designed for youth and families. See the park newspaper distributed at entrance stations and look for Ranger Programs. Child-centered programs are at Mammoth Hot Springs, Old Faithful, Canyon Village, and Fishing Bridge.

Take a Walk in the Park

Do you want to explore the park with your child without a guide? Yellowstone has more than 1,000 miles of backcountry trails. You would need several summers to experience the entire park by foot. Start with short, educational, and exciting walks that will inspire your child to want to return for more challenging experiences. Consider your child's limits. Here are some short walks that are entertaining and educational, revealing to children the wonders of Yellowstone.

EASY SHORT HIKES FOR KIDS

Mammoth

Wraith Falls, 1 mile round-trip. The trailhead is 5 miles east of Mammoth Hot Springs along the Grand Loop Road. Look for American dippers feeding and flying at the falls.

Upper Geyser Basin

Upper Geyser Basin, 3 miles round-trip. Leave from Old Faithful and follow the pathway northwest past many outstanding geothermal features until you arrive at the Morning Glory Pool. Retrace your steps or make a loop by taking the boardwalk by Grotto Geyser toward Geyser Hill. Your child will marvel at the astounding abundance of features.

Mystic Falls, 2 miles round-trip. The trail leaves from the west end of Biscuit Basin and winds through a lodgepole pine forest burned in 1988. After about 0.5-mile, it enters unburned areas and begins to follow the Little Firehole River. Mystic Falls is a spectacle as it splashes 70 feet over a series of ledges.

Lake

Storm Point Trail, 2.3 miles round-trip. The trailhead is 3 miles east of Fishing Bridge along the East Entrance Road. Walk through sagebrush and an old-growth spruce-fir forest, and arrive at the south end of Yellowstone Lake, where centuries of southerly winds have piled dunes high along the shore. Marmots are often seen at the rocky outcrop of Storm Point. The loop trail takes you through a lodgepole pine forest and back to your car.

Natural Bridge, 3 miles round-trip. You and your child will marvel at this geologic rarity. It took the creek more than 70,000 years to carve the feature. It's an easy, mostly flat walk through lodgepole, spruce, and fir forests along Bridge Creek.

Canyon

North Rim Trail, 3 miles one-way. Begin at the Brink of the Upper Falls parking area, 2 miles south of Canyon Village. You can walk the entire 3 miles to Inspiration Point or turn back at any point. This trail is paved along some stretches. It offers many viewpoints of the Lower Falls and Grand Canyon of the Yellowstone.

Madison

Harlequin Lake, 1 mile round-trip. The trailhead is 1.5 miles west of Madison Junction along the West Entrance Road.

Artists Paint Pots, 1 mile round-trip. This delightful small geyser basin in an area most visitors drive past. Bubbling colorful mud will challenge the imagination of young and old.

Lamar Valley

Trout Lake, 1.2 miles round-trip. This is one of the most beautiful lake settings in Yellowstone. Surrounded by forests and cliffs, Trout Lake is a surprise treat. It is a landscape that inspires renewal, a good place to encourage your child to reflect on the wonders of Yellowstone.

Area Trail Guides

Area trail guides are available at the visitor centers throughout the park. A 50-cent donation to the Yellowstone Association is requested. The guides have trail maps, as well as natural and cultural heritage information.

- *Mammoth Hot Springs Trail Guide: Including Lower Terraces and Upper Terrace Drive*
- *Old Faithful Historic District: A Brief History & Walking Tour*
- *Upper Geyser Basin*
- *Canyon Area Trail Guide: Featuring the Grand Canyon of the Yellowstone River, Including North Rim Drive and South Rim Drive*
- *Norris Geyser Basin Trail Guide: Including Porcelain and Back Basins*
- *West Thumb Geyser Basin Trail Guide: Including Fishing Cone and Thumb Paint Pots*

Skip Rocks

Wave action for thousands of years has smoothed rocks into perfectly flat silver-dollar-size skipping stones at the shores of Yellowstone Lake and Lewis Lake. Look for abundant stones along the shoreline of Yellowstone Lake at Mary Bay, Sedge Bay, Bluff Point, and Gull Point Drive. On calm days, Lewis Lake's glassy waters make it an ideal lake for rock skipping. Find a good pullout anywhere along the South Entrance Road.

Read Aloud

Be prepared. A rainy day or a lull in activities gives you an opportunity to read a book with your child. Many entertaining and informative books are available at the Yellowstone Natural History Association bookstore in Gardiner and at retailers and visitor centers throughout the park. Pick some that you want to read and that will give your child a better understanding of Yellowstone National Park's heritage.

Plan ahead, and build the anticipation phase of their holiday. Contact the Yellowstone Association at www.yellowstoneassociation.org, and order books that will delight your child. You can read to them as you travel to Yellowstone. Here is a sample of the dozens of available books that will complement their experiences in the park:

- *Be a Park Ranger,* Robert Rath (ages 2 and up)
- *Black Bear Babies!* (ages 0-3)
- *Grizzly Babies!* (ages 0-3)
- *Moose Babies!* (ages 0-3)
- *Yellowstone Babies!* (ages 0-3)
- *Mountain Goat Babies!* (ages 0-3)
- *Yellowstone's Hot Legends and Cool Myths,* Robert Rath (ages 8 to 12)
- *Who Pooped in the Park? Yellowstone National Park,* Gary Robson (ages 5 to 8)
- *Going to Yellowstone,* Peter and Connie Roop (ages 8 to 12)
- *Fascinating Facts About Old Faithful,* Susan Scofield (ages 10 to adult)
- *How Do Bears Sleep?* E. J. Bird (ages 2 and up)
- *Lost in the Woods,* Carl R. Sams II and Jean Stoick (ages 2 and up)
- *Silvertip: A Year in the Life of a Yellowstone Grizzly,* Ted Rechlin (ages 5 to 8)
- *The Yellowstone Kid,* Johnny Boyd (ages 2 and up)

Go for a Cruise

Take a one-hour scenic cruise out of Bridge Bay on Yellowstone Lake aboard the *Lake Queen II.* The cruise is offered several times daily during the busy summer season. You can also rent motorboats with all the necessary gear, including life vests, at the marina. Go in the morning when the water is calm, before afternoon winds stir up waves.

Ride a Horse

Give your 8-year and older children a sense of what it must have been like to see Yellowstone National Park before automobiles became the primary source of transportation. Rides are one and two hours through sagebrush and forested landscapes. Outfitters offer horseback rides at Mammoth, Canyon, and Tower-Roosevelt.

Tallyho!
Imagine that you are in the Old West riding a stagecoach to your destination. Climb aboard a replica Tally-ho coach, similar to those used in Yellowstone's early years. Rides last one hour from the Roosevelt corral.

Attend an Old West Cookout
What was it like to be a cowboy at the end of a long day of wrangling cattle? Get a feel of what it was like to have dinner around a campfire, with music, storytelling, and cowboy-style cooking. Reservations are required for this popular family activity. Wagons leave from Roosevelt each afternoon.

Reflect
Today's fast-paced, gadget-filled lifestyle is busy with distractions. Yellowstone National Park presents wonderful opportunities to take a deep breath and reconnect with the natural world. Find a quiet, peaceful spot. Challenge your child to sit in solitude for 5 or 10 minutes. (Try it yourself!) Ask them to think about what they hear, smell, and see. Encourage them to write or draw about the experience and what their senses revealed to them. As they settle in for the night, ask your child to reflect on what they liked about the day's activities.

View the Night Sky
One August night many years ago, I was returning to Mammoth alone on the road through Gardners Hole. I was enthralled by the countless stars above me. A sudden flash revealed a long, waving, green and blue curtain reaching from the northern horizon to the sky's apex. I stopped at the Swan Lake pullout, got out of my car, and watched an aurora borealis so encompassing that my recollection is vivid 20 years later.

Most Americans live in cities and suburbs. Living under the glow of urban lights, children do not experience the excitement of seeing the Milky Way, meteor showers, or summer constellations. Yellowstone's dark nighttime skies allow you to stargaze with your child. Do it on your own, or attend one of the nighttime programs offered in cooperation with the Museum of the Rockies and the Southwest Montana Astronomical Society. Hear star stories, identify constellations, and view the night sky through telescopes. The night sky inspires awe in a child, and its mysteries are brought to light when a family member takes the time to share in the discovery.

BEST PLACES TO LISTEN TO MUSIC

Gather with family and friends to enjoy music after a long day of touring the park. Throughout the summer, performing artists play at venues in and around the park. The two most popular places in Yellowstone are at Lake Hotel and Old Faithful Inn. Evening performances include a piano or a string quartet. Find a comfortable seat, order a drink, take in the music, and reflect on the day's adventures.

Jim Peaco, National Park Service

BEST SUNRISE AND SUNSET SPOTS

Richard Lake, National Park Service

While touring Yellowstone in the early morning or late afternoon, you may chance upon a kaleidoscope of colors in the eastern or western sky. Multi-hued sunrises and sunsets frame the landscape, inspiring awe and reflection. Here are some places where locals find great views at dawn and day's end.

Sunrise

The best sunrise views are from unobstructed vistas, such as mountain peaks. But this requires that you begin hiking well before dawn to reach your destination, which I do not recommend in bear country. A good option is watching the sunrise from the West Thumb Geyser Basin. Walking is minimal from the parking lot. Old Faithful Geyser and its neighbors in the Upper Geyser Basin also make for memorable backdrops at sunrise and sunset.

Sunset

The best sunset view is from the Yellowstone Lake Butte Overlook. Arrive early for the breathtaking views of Yellowstone Lake before you, and the Grand Tetons to the south. No hiking is involved. The overlook turnoff is about 8 miles east of Fishing Bridge on the East Entrance Road.

ICONIC SUBJECTS TO PHOTOGRAPH

William S. Keller, National Park Service

If this is your first trip to Yellowstone National Park, you likely will be taking pictures of everything that grabs your interest. Here is a list of the iconic images that you may want to capture and share with your family and friends back home.

- A Yellowstone National Park entrance sign
- Old Faithful Geyser erupting
- Old Faithful Inn, interior and exterior
- Grand Canyon of the Yellowstone; Artist Point is an excellent spot
- Lower Falls of the Yellowstone from Red Rock Point or Artist Point
- Mammoth Hot Springs, Minerva Terrace, and the Liberty Cap
- Grand Prismatic Spring
- Hayden Valley for elk and bison

The best times to photograph these features are before 10 a.m. and after 4 p.m. in order to avoid deep contrasting shadows. Many professional photographers look for clear skies the morning following a cold front. You can also get great results in the early morning or late afternoon by positioning an erupting geyser between you and the sun.

BEST PLACES TO TAKE A GROUP PORTRAIT

Record your visit to Yellowstone for posterity: take a group portrait. Most visitors look for the most memorable and iconic locations for picture backdrops. Popular spots include any of the park entrance signs, the Continental Divide sign along the road between Old Faithful and West Thumb, Mammoth Hot Springs Lower Terrace, Roosevelt Arch, Artist Point at Canyon, and in front of Old Faithful while it erupts.

Make sure that everyone is in the photograph. You'll find plenty of visitors eager to snap the shutter for you.

BEST PLACES TO PEOPLE WATCH

The themes of Yellowstone are universal. You come to Yellowstone to seek the serenity of nature, manifested in the park's surreal geology

Jay Elhard, National Park Service

and wild animals. So does everyone around you. Your experiences are shared.

How do others react to these wonders? Shared experiences can add pleasure to your visit. There are three places where large numbers of people gather and spend a lot of time: the lobby of the Old Faithful Inn, the Old Faithful Geyser viewing area, and the Upper Geyser Basin.

Old Faithful Inn Lobby

Find a comfortable place to sit and watch the procession that follows an Old Faithful Geyser eruption. Listen to many languages, and absorb some of the excitement of fellow travelers as they enter the lobby for the first time. Watch visitors explore the interior of the inn. The best times to interact with others are mid-morning, late afternoon, and early evening.

Old Faithful Geyser Viewing Area

Arrive early at the boardwalk viewing area to get a good spot and to watch as others survey the scene for the best places to see Old Faithful. Notice how the conversations get louder as visitors' anticipation grows before the eruption.

Jim Peaco, National Park Service

Upper Geyser Basin

The paved walkway from Old Faithful Geyser to Morning Glory Pool is an excellent place to enjoy people as they hike, ride bicycles, jog, walk as families, and gather in groups. The pathway is an easy walk. You will encounter large numbers of people from all over the United States and many foreign countries who stroll here to see the fantastic geothermal features. Listen to their various accents and languages. It is a good place to practice your foreign language skills.

BEST BOOKS ABOUT YELLOWSTONE

Good Reads

- *A Ranger's Guide to Yellowstone Day Hikes,* Roger Anderson and Carol Shively Anderson
- *A Farcountry Field Guide: Yellowstone and Grand Teton National Parks,* Kurt F. Johnson
- *Yellowstone's Rebirth by Fire: Rising from the Ashes of the 1988 Wildfires,* Karen Reinhart
- *The Geysers of Yellowstone,* T. Scott Bryan
- *Wolf: Return to Yellowstone,* Michael Milstein
- *Moose Droppings,* William J. Lewis
- *Portrait of Yellowstone: Land of Geysers and Grizzlies,* photos by David Peterson
- *Yellowstone Wild and Beautiful,* Fred Pflughoft
- *Yellowstone Impressions,* Fred Pflughoft

Kids' Books

- *Going to Yellowstone,* Peter and Connie Roop
- *Bison Babies!* Donald M. Jones
- *Black Bear Babies!* Donald M. Jones
- *Grizzly Babies!* Henry H. Holdsworth
- *Wolf Babies!* Lisa and Mike Husar
- *Who Pooped in the Park? Yellowstone National Park,* Gary Robson
- *Yellowstone's Hot Legends and Cool Myths,* Robert Rath

RESOURCES

There are many opportunities for you to learn about the natural and cultural heritage of the Greater Yellowstone Region. The National Park Service, private foundations, and concessionaires offer many services and opportunities that will enhance your visit. Outside the park, other discovery centers and museums help tell the Yellowstone area story.

General Park Information
Yellowstone National Park
P.O. Box 168
Yellowstone National Park
Wyoming 82190-0168
www.nps.gov/yell
(307) 344-7381

Campgrounds
All National Park Service campgrounds are on a first-come, first-served basis. NPS campgrounds are Mammoth, Norris, Tower Fall, Indian Creek, Pebble Creek, Slough Creek, and Lewis Lake.

Reservations are needed for campgrounds operated by Xanterra Parks and Resorts:

- Madison, Canyon, Grant Village, Bridge Bay, and Fishing Bridge RV Park:
www.yellowstonenationalparklodges.com
toll-free (866) 439-7375 or (307) 344-7311

All USDA Forest Service campgrounds in Bridger-Teton, Caribou-Targhee, Gallatin, and Shoshone National Forests are on a first-come, first-served basis. Available facilities and fees for camping vary. For information on camping and cabin rentals on specific forests, see:

- Bridger-Teton National Forest:
www.fs.usda.gov/activity/btnf/recreation/camping-cabins
- Caribou-Targhee National Forest:
www.fs.usda.gov/detail/r4/recreation/?cid=stelprdb5381480
- Gallatin National Forest:
www.fs.usda.gov/activity/gallatin/recreation/camping-cabins
- Shoshone National Forest:
www.fs.usda.gov/activity/shoshone/recreation/camping-cabins

Jim Peaco, National Park Service

Visitor Centers, Museums, and Other Attractions

Yellowstone Association
The Yellowstone Association has been the park's nonprofit educational partner since 1933, offering in-depth educational programs and memberships that support the park's educational projects, publications, and exhibits. Visit the Yellowstone Association Headquarters and store in Gardiner for up-to-date information about membership, programs, and wildlife sightings. www.yellowstoneassociation.org; (406) 848-2400.

Yellowstone Park Foundation
The foundation's mission is to fund projects and programs that protect, preserve, and enhance the park's natural and cultural resources, and the visitor experience of the park. www.ypf.org; (406) 586-6303.

Many opportunities exist to enrich your holiday outside of Yellowstone National Park.

The Museum of the Rockies
BOZEMAN, MONTANA
The museum is located in the heart of the Rocky Mountains in Bozeman, Montana, just 90 minutes north of Yellowstone National Park. The museum showcases one of the largest and most important dinosaur collections in the world and is a "must-see" destination for any visitor to the area. www.museumoftherockies.org; (406) 994-2251.

Buffalo Bill Center of the West
CODY, WYOMING
Positioning the story of Cody's life within the context of the history and myth of the American West, the museum documents how, in an age without television or motion pictures, and under the persona of "Buffalo Bill," Cody became the world's foremost communicator about the history, promise, and enduring spirit of the American West.

In addition to documenting the life and interests of William F. Cody, and the history and operations of Buffalo Bill's Wild West Show, the museum's collection interprets the history of the American cowboy, dude ranching, western conservation, frontier entrepreneurship, and the source of our concepts about the West. www.centerofthewest.org; (307) 587-4771.

Yellowstone Gateway Museum
LIVINGSTON, MONTANA
This year-round museum is located an hour north of Gardiner, Montana, and interprets Park County and its relationship to Yellowstone National Park. Visitors experience four exhibit rooms housed in a historic schoolhouse that focus on the themes of native cultures, expeditions, transportation, and pioneer artifacts and stories as well as changing exhibits. The museum includes Yellowstone historic vehicles, a caboose, a one-room schoolhouse, and a research center. www.yellowstonegatewaymuseum.org; (406) 222-4184.

Museum of the Mountain Man
PINEDALE, WYOMING
This museum presents a visual and interpretative experience into the romantic era of the 1800s mountain man and provides a comprehensive overview of the western fur trade's historical significance. www.museumofthemountainman.com; toll-free (877) 686-6266 or (307) 367-4101.

Grand Teton National Park
MOOSE, WYOMING
Rising above a scene rich with extraordinary wildlife, pristine lakes, and alpine terrain, the Teton Range stands monument to the people who fought to protect it. These are mountains of the imagination, mountains that led to the creation of Grand Teton National Park, where you can explore more than 200 miles of trails, float the Snake River, or enjoy the serenity of this remarkable place. www.nps.gov/grte; (307) 739-3300.

John D. Rockefeller, Jr. Memorial Parkway
MOOSE, WYOMING
The parkway connects Grand Teton and Yellowstone National Parks. John D. Rockefeller, Jr. made significant contributions to several national parks including Grand Teton, Acadia, Great Smoky Mountains, and Virgin Islands. In 1972, Congress dedicated a 24,000-acre parcel of land as John D. Rockefeller, Jr. Memorial Parkway to recognize his generosity and foresight. www.nps.gov/grte/jodr.htm; (307) 739-3300.

Earthquake Lake and Visitor Center

WEST YELLOWSTONE, MONTANA

Earthquake Lake Visitor Center is 24 miles northwest of West Yellowstone on U.S. Highway 287. Operated by the USDA Forest Service, the center provides a panoramic view of the mountain that fell and the lake that was formed. The facility has interpretive displays on earthquakes and plate tectonics, and a working seismograph. In the observatory, scheduled movies and talks explain the story of the "the night the earth moved"—the 1959 Hebgen Lake earthquake. www.fs.fed.us.rl/gallatin; (406) 682-7620.

Beartooth Scenic Byway

RED LODGE, MONTANA

Beartooth Scenic Byway is Wyoming's highest paved primary road, cresting on 10,947-foot Beartooth Pass. The traveling CBS journalist Charles Kuralt once called it "the most beautiful drive in America." From Red Lodge, Montana, U.S. Highway 212 climbs to alpine tundra and the pass. The 67-mile route is known for its astonishing beauty. As you might imagine, the road is seasonal due to the short summers at this altitude. For current information on road conditions, contact Friends of Beartooth Pass, Red Lodge, Montana, email: info@beartoothhighway.com; (307) 250-1510.

Pahaska Tepee

CODY, WYOMING

Pahaska Tepee was Buffalo Bill's historic hunting lodge, built in 1894. The lodge is just outside Yellowstone's East Entrance on U.S. Highway 14/16/20 and is open for viewing during the busy summer season. Today, Pahaska Teepee also includes modern accommodations, a restaurant, and a store that are open from May to October. www.pahaska.com; toll-free (800) 628-7791 or (307) 527-7701.

Grizzly & Wolf Discovery Center

WEST YELLOWSTONE, MONTANA

The center's mission is to provide visitors to the Yellowstone area an opportunity to observe, understand, and appreciate grizzly bears and gray wolves. You will find the center at the West Entrance of the park. Open 365 days a year, the center offers a variety of programs on bears, wolves, and birds of prey. www.grizzlydiscoveryctr.com; toll-free (800) 257-2570 or (406) 646-7001.

Yellowstone Historic Center Museum
WEST YELLOWSTONE, MONTANA
The museum is in the former Union Pacific Railroad Depot where for several decades visitors from the southwest disembarked for their Yellowstone holiday. Today, the building houses a collection of artifacts, historic vehicles, important documents, and photographs of bygone times. www.yellowstonehistoriccenter.org; (406) 646-1100.

Glacier National Park
WEST GLACIER, MONTANA
Have you ever seen a glacier? Would you like to experience the American Alps? Known as the Crown of the Continent, Glacier has pristine forests, alpine tundra meadows, rugged mountains, and spectacular lakes. With more than 700 miles of trails, Glacier is a hiker's paradise for adventurous visitors seeking wilderness and solitude. Relive the days of old through historic chalets, lodges, transportation, and stories of Native Americans. Glacier is about a day's drive north of Gardiner or West Yellowstone. Explore Glacier National Park and discover what awaits you. www.nps.gov/glac; (406) 888-7800.

National Park Service

Jim Peaco, National Park Service

ABOUT THE AUTHOR

Alan Leftridge was a seasonal naturalist in Yellowstone and a ranger in the Mission Mountains Wilderness in Montana. He earned a B.S. in biology at the University of Central Missouri, a secondary teaching credential from the University of Montana, and a Ph.D. in science education and cultural geography at Kansas State University. He taught high school science in West Yellowstone, science education at Miami University, and environmental studies at Humboldt State University. For 20 years, he was the executive editor of the Interpreter *and* Legacy *magazines. His books include* Best of Glacier National Park, Glacier Day Hikes, Seeley-Swan Day Hikes, Going to Glacier, *and* Interpretive Writing. *Alan lives in the Swan Valley of northwestern Montana.*